THE CLASSIC MEMOIR OF A
BLEW-THE-WHIST

JACK NASTY-FACE

WILLIAM ROBINSON

INTRODUCED BY
PETER BUTT

BLACKWATTLE
PRESS

First published in 1836 as Nautical Economy or Forecastle Recollections of Events During the Last War.

By William Robinson

Restored and Introduced by Peter Butt

Published by Blackwattle Press, Sydney, Australia

Publisher: Peter Butt

Associate Publisher: Sarah Staveley

www.blackwattlepress.com.au

ISBN: 978-0-9923252-6-8

Contents

Introduction
Dedication
Preface
Advertisement
1. Entering the Navy
2. Preparing for Battle
3. The advantage of learning to dance
4. The danger of giving too much power into the hands of young officers
5. Conjugal affection and heroinism of a French Female
6. The Day after the Battle
7. Arrival at Gibraltar
8. Safe arrival at Home
9. Blockade of Sourdeaux and Rochefort
10. Engagement with a French Squadron
11. Joining the Blockade off Cadiz
12. In England once again
13. Pay-day on Board
14. To Sea again
15. Postscript
16. The Different Modes of Punishment in the British Navy
17. Flogging through the Fleet
18. Running the Gauntlet
19. Flogging at the Gangway or on the Quarter-Deck
20. Starting
21. Gagging
22. Observations on Impressment

Introduction

If history is written by the victors, the history of 19th Century Britain is indelibly linked to 'the wooden walls of Old England' — the Royal Navy. In the 1820s, numerous former Naval officers put quill to paper to recount their great adventures and the victories that helped extend the British Empire. Invariably, they credited the British seamen in every part of the world for ‘enlarging the domains of religion and civilisation’ and offering ‘the oppressed asylum and fighting the scourge of tyranny.’

In reality, life on board for many a common seaman was marked by oppression and brutal punishment, meted out by officers and sanctioned by the parliament.

For a sailor from the lower deck to write of his experiences in battle or to criticise the Royal Navy and its harsh disciplinary practices was virtually unheard of until 1836, when William Robinson published his powerful and controversial book, *A Nautical Economy; Or Forecastle Recollections of Events During the Last War.*

I first came upon William Robinson by accident. While researching my family tree, I found a newspaper obituary for my great aunt, Catherine Heagney, which told of her pride in her mother's father, William Wells Robinson, who had "accompanied Captain Cook on his voyage to Australia in 1770 and had fought with Lord Nelson at Trafalgar."

I had no recollection of my family ever mentioning a forebear named Robinson, so I delved into my mother's family line and discovered that William Wells Robinson, born in 1787 in Middlesex, was my fourth great-grandfather.

As Cook 'discovered' Australia seventeen years before William's birth, Aunt Catherine had clearly fallen victim to the all-too-common 'family myth'. However, the possibility that William Robinson was at Trafalgar set me on a trail of discovery.

Numerous sources confirmed that Robinson was indeed at the famous sea battle aboard HMS Revenge, a 74-gun, third-rate, ship-of-the-line that sailed with Admiral Collingwood's column.

Back in 2000, I directed a four-part documentary series for British, U.S. and Australian broadcasters about the dramatic history of the battleship, which until the nuclear age, was the most powerful and deadly machine ever built. With the input of naval experts, we explored the subject of Admiral Horatio Nelson's victory at Cape Trafalgar, which saved Britain from the threat of invasion by Napoleon.

Considering the terrifying intensity of the battle, I could now only marvel that one of my forebears, at the age of seventeen, had participated in such close-range and ferocious fighting and had survived unscathed.

My research took an intriguing turn when I learned that William Robinson, an ordinary seaman, had authored and self-published a controversial book about his experiences during the Trafalgar campaign and other actions, including the notoriously unsuccessful attack on the French fleet in the 'Battle of Basque Roads' and the disastrous Walcheren campaign in 1809.

Robinson also delved into areas of naval life endured by the ordinary seaman, especially the draconian disciplinary system and the use of impressment, or 'press-ganging' - the capture and forcing of men into naval service.

Robinson also wrote of the various tactics men used to escape from service. Understandably, he didn't mention that in 1811, after six years of service, he had also deserted. In a time of war, desertion was a hanging offence.

Coincidentally, his 'run' appears to have coincided with his meeting young Elizabeth Pearce, whom he married in February of the following year. As a landlubber, William took up his father's trade of shoemaking. Elizabeth gave birth to two girls but died following the second birth.

In 1823, William changed his occupation to that of news-vendor and stationer. In December 1825, he married again to a widow named Elizabeth Vallejo. In the early 1830s, the family moved to a substantial, brick-built house at 9 Staining Lane, Cheapside, a few hundred metres from London Wall. The shingle on the door read *Robinson's Newspaper-office*.

After hours, William began penning a memoir of his service in the Royal Navy. It was a dangerous move; he'd prudently kept his head low for over two decades but was now prepared to resurface and deliberately tug the Lion's tail.

Predicting a less than favourable response from the Navy, Robinson chose a nom de plume, 'Jack Nasty-Face'. The book first appeared in London bookshops in January 1836, selling for three shillings 'stitched in a wrapper' or 'bound in cloth' for an extra sixpence. As a newspaper vendor, Robinson apparently appreciated the value of publicity, advertising his book in select newspapers and dispatching copies to their editors.

The first review appeared on 24 January 1836 in *Bell's New Weekly Messenger*:

> *This is a plain narrative of facts - facts of an amusing and of a heartrending nature. Every Englishman should read it, and the members of the legislature more particularly.*

Bell's New Weekly Messenger followed up with a more detailed book review in its next edition. The reviewer was especially disturbed by the descriptions of the copious injustices and cruelties that were meted out by Royal Naval officers:

We had imagined that nothing could be more cruel than the mode of punishment adopted in our Army; but a little publication has been laid before us, disclosing atrocities more horrible than the worst enormities that have ever been perpetrated by military tyrants, and which are represented by common occurrences in the British Navy. The description of the modes of torture practiced during the last war, by one who has evidently beheld them inflicted and perhaps had some of them inflicted upon himself, is frightful and appalling; and had the narrator added that some of the miserable fellows doomed by a naval villain to such a devilish punishment as that of a "flogging through the fleet" preferring death at the yard-arm, had attempted to rid the world of their diabolical persecutor, we should have deemed the impulse a very natural one, and have felt no regret."

The *Bell's* reviewer suggested that if the British Parliament wished men to volunteer to serve in times of emergency, it should in intervene.

It makes the heart sick to read of such bloody work. And these are practices in the British Navy! The brave fellows who man the wooden walls of old England, are subject to these tortures! The men who performed such prodigies of valor in the last war, many of them, tortured in this infernal way, by the hell-hounds placed in authority over them. In the event of another war, and with these appalling facts before them, can it be expected that brave and worthy men will voluntarily enter service? Certainly not. This is surely then, a subject for Parliamentary interference? No negro-slavery can be worse than seaman-slavery, no tyranny greater than the tyranny of naval officers, and we trust that some spirited representative of the people will bring the whole subject before the Legislature.

The reaction in naval circles was far from complimentary. *The Naval and Military Gazette and Weekly Chronicle of the United Service* of 13 February 1836 even doubted that it had come from the pen of an ordinary sailor:

> *The intention of the author is evidently to depreciate the Naval Service, to make the seamen discontented with their state, and to narrate incidents of no interest, solely for the purpose of introducing practices which have long been abolished afloat. We are only astonished that the writer could find a publisher. The book is undeserving of any notice. The "Forecastle Recollections" never could have been written by a thorough seaman; they carry with them every evidence emanating from the mind of "a sea lawyer," or "Lord Mayor's man".*

The term '*Lord Mayor's man*' came into use in the mid-1790s to describe a youth from a good family, often distinguished by the fashionable cut of his civilian clothing, who had been found in bawdy houses or drunk in the street and was sentenced to Naval Service to set him on the 'straight and narrow'. Often these were educated men who were beneficial to the shipmates in the lower ranks yet made captains nervous, as they were more likely to see injustices and organise reactions against them.

Robinson was not a *Lord Mayor's man*, but judging by his literary writing and engaging storytelling, he was undoubtedly educated and, therefore, ultimately dangerous. Indeed, the release of *Nautical Economy* could not have come at a worse time for the Royal Navy, which was about to embark on a recruiting drive.

Two months after Nautical Economy's release, the Lancaster Gazette of 19 March, 1936, reported that:

> *...orders had been sent round by the Lords of the Admiralty for the immediate enlistment, at the various depots of Liverpool, Portsmouth, etc., of able bodied seaman to equip fifteen ships in her Majesty's service, which were instantly being put in commission, and whose destination was supposed to be the Mediterranean.*

Coincidentally or on purpose, the *Lancaster Gazette* featured an extract from Robinson's book on the same page, in which his Jack Nasty-Face describes the terrible reality of battle, which would have done little to encourage naval volunteers.

Besides the Navy's negative response, I wondered if there had been repercussions for William Robinson. According to his descendant, Beverley Towns, in her fine book *Surrey to Singleton: a tribute to William and Elizabeth Robinson*, the government arrested the book's printer, George Parsonage, and endeavoured to find the author.

While Robinson had disguised his authorship, the first edition of the book bore his name as publisher and even noted his address: 9 Staining-lane, Wood-street, Cheapside. One would expect the authorities to have enquired with the publisher before harassing the humble printer. In her book, Beverley Towns suggests that: *'In 1839, William's plight became acute, and he turned his attention to the availability of passage to Australia...'*

Indeed, on June 1, 1839, William Robinson, his wife Elizabeth and their three children departed England on *HMS Neptune*. They sailed as free settlers halfway around the world to Sydney, New South Wales. By the end of the year, they were living in a small timber cottage on an isolated 2000-acre property in the Hunter Valley, 180 km from Sydney. They would never see home again.

To my mind, such a move would have been years in the planning and, therefore, must have been prompted by officialdom's response to his book, not only because it contained unreserved criticism of the all-powerful British Navy but because Robinson was also a naval deserter.

Beverley Towns uncovered intriguing evidence in Neptune's manifest: rather than 'Robinson', William travelled under the name of 'Robertson'. This wasn't simply a spelling error. William and his wife, Elizabeth, are recorded separately in other immigration documents as 'Robertson'. Moreover, William is listed as a 'shoemaker,' an occupation he had abandoned over a decade and a half earlier. This evidence supports Beverly Towns' assertion that William feared the authorities. William and his family ultimately settled in Singleton, New South Wales. He died in 1846 at the age of fifty-nine.

In a presentation at the Museum of Democracy in Canberra, another of William Robinson's descendants, Sharon Towns, spoke of her pride in her fourth great-grandfather's "creation and literary legacy, his compassion and acumen, conscious of righteousness and justice during a time of conflict and oppression and particularly courageous enough to criticise his government and institutions for their treatment of fellow countrymen. I like to think that William represents that individual voice speaking up for social justice and the human rights of the day. Through a sense of moral duty, he 'outed bad behaviour', bullying and enslavement within the British Navy to a wider audience. And that while such published accounts and statements were considered treasonous and punishable by death, he was compelled to risk personal safety. I also believe that he represents the ideal that an individual voice can catalyse change for the improvement of many. And so we can arrive at contemporary parallels that challenge us all to determine our moral centre and the individual courage to express and defend it. I feel fortunate my ancestor had the foresight to emigrate ahead of the law; one wonders if contemporaneously his family wouldn't be considered political boat refugees."

William Wells Robinson's astonishing tale has long been out of print. While an electronic edition is available, sections of text are missing. This new print edition includes reviews of the book which followed its release in 1836 and another a century later.

Peter Butt

Sydney, Australia

Note: The following text contains original spelling

NAUTICAL ECONOMY

or

FORECASTLE RECOLLECTIONS

of

EVENTS DURING THE LAST WAR
DEDICATED TO THE
BRAVE TARS OF OLD ENGLAND

BY A SAILOR,

POLITELY CALLED BY THE OFFICERS OF THE NAVY,

JACK NASTY-FACE.

" *Be ye my Witness that I lie not.* "

PUBLISHED BY WILLIAM ROBINSON,
9, STAINING LANE, WOOD STREET, CHEAPSIDE.
Price 3s. in Wrapper, and 3s.6d. Bound in Cloth.
[Entered at Stationers' Hall.]

Dedication

TO THE BRAVE TARS OF OLD ENGLAND

My brother Seamen and old Shipmates,

The British Public has of late been amused with various accounts of naval affairs, by quarter-deck and epaulette authors, and now one of yourselves ventures to come forward, and give his yarn of the matter, with a forecastle experience. D'ye-see, I cannot, like some of these great cabin and high-flown gentle men-writers, show much reading, by dressing up the figure-head and stern gallery of my work, with quotations from Admiral Horner, Commodore Virgil, or Captain Caesar, as I do not understand their lingo; but I can speak the truth with any man; and shall unfurl a foremast man's log of wants on board a ship, and appeal to you as my witnesses, that what I state is the truth, the whole truth, aye, and nothing but the truth; as they swear you on a court-martial.

Without paying either yourselves, or myself an unjust compliment, I do think, and believe you will agree with me, that a statement, written on a seaman's chest below, is likely to be as accurate, to what passes 'tween decks, as the flowery display coming from a cabin dilettante; who may be either scribbling and splicing the odds and end together of the miracles he has seen, or, thrusting himself forward to show his (perhaps noble) friends and relatives, that he has not had a speaking trumpet in his hand, and walked the quarter-deck for nothing. Yes, my brother seamen, I say, more likely to be accurate: for you all know that the man in the foretop can give a better description of what passes in the horizon, than the gallant observer, how ever gifted by education, whose eyes rise but a little above the drum-head of the capstan.

The order of the present day, on land, it seems is reform:—then why should the sea-service have its imperfections remain unattended to? To bring about, there fore, a reform in that all-important department of the state, it is, that without being considered an improper intruder, I may be suffered to offer for public consideration my mite of information; trusting it may be useful to obtain so desirable an object; and I hope that whenever my country's welfare is at stake, and my king's happiness or honour, I may bear in mind the last signal of my noble and ever to be lamented brave commander, Lord Nelson, “England expects each man will do his duty,” and so on this occasion I have endeavoured to do mine.

Without therefore fatiguing you, by throwing out a long yarn of address, I shall let my pen turn in, counting on your honest hearts to be the stanchion of my veracity. With sincerely wishing you health and happiness here, which, is, life's *pleasant* weather, let me hope,

When HE who ALL commands,

Shall give, to call life's crew together,

The word, to pipe all hands:

that we may, in answering to the quarter bill,

find ourselves stationed in THE MAIN TOP OF GLORY.

Preface

In this narrative the reader must not calculate upon meeting with high flown language or flowers of rhetoric; for the author like many others, has had a very slender education, yet he will endeavour to make himself understood, even with the limited means he possesses. As it may be gratifying to some, nay, many may wish to know something of the author, I therefore unhesitatingly state, that my father was an honest tradesman, but in humble circumstances, as a shoemaker.

I was very early put to the business, which my roving mind would not suffer me to pursue; and in one of the vagaries of my youth, on the 9th May, 1805, I repaired to the rendezvous which was opened on Tower-hill, and there offered my services to his Majesty. The regulating officer seeing me with an apron on, suspected that I was a runaway apprentice, but I soon undeceived him, and I was sent on board the receiving ship then laying off the Tower; to begin a career of life, which fancy had moulded into a variety of shapes, gilded by hope, with fortune, honour, and happiness, all in full view.

The language in which this work will be coiled up, may by some, seem to partake too much of the forecastle academy for it will be recollected, that I was never on the quarter-deck but when ordered on duty, and was only permitted to say, "Aye, Aye, sir," when spoken to, at the same time touching the rim of my castor, with all due respect to my officers.

To the seaman, much of this work will appear trifling, but to the landsman, it will give information, which may be useful, as it will be instructive, describing minutely a sailor's life on board a ship. I shall speak in plain language on the subject of impressment and naval punishments; and as these subjects, it is expected, will shortly I hope engage legislative attention, perhaps the facts it will contain may meet the eye of those interested; and thus far I may have helped to serve my country, as my anxious desire is to live and witness the adoption of some other system resorted to, for manning the navy, and showing obedience, than impressment, and unnecessary cruel punishment fiction shall, in no page, find its way in the catalogue of occurrences; I have taken truth for my pilot, and, without fear do I throw myself on the candour of a generous public.

J.N.

Advertisement

The Reader will be pleased to observe, that, although several gallant Captains in the navy have lately sent out some cruizers, upon a speculative construction, with fine gilt upper works fore and aft, and gaudily fitted up on the inside, intended no doubt to join the Yacht Club, and as such, must be much admired; yet it is believed that this little vessel will out-sail them all, and be classed A.1. in Paternoster Row; being well adapted for a foreign station, the channel service, or the coasting trade. It is pilot-boat built, being very sharp, with a good deal of deadrise, and is schooner rigged: the fore-mast, is of patriotism and loyalty, and her main-mast of truth; and well stored with luxuries, as may be seen from the following account of stowage on board.

Entering the Navy

Whatever may be said about this boasted land of liberty, whenever a youth resorts to a receiving ship for shelter and hospitality, he, from that moment, must take leave of the liberty to speak, or to act; he may think, but he must confine his thoughts to the hold of his mind, and never suffer them to escape the hatchway of utterance. On being sent on board the receiving ship, it was for the first time I began to repent of the rash step I had taken, but it was of no avail, submission to the events of fate was my only alternative, murmuring or remonstrating, I soon found, would be folly.

After having been examined by the doctor, and reported seaworthy, I was ordered down to the hold, where I remained all night (9th May, 1805,) with my companions in wretchedness, and the rats running over us in numbers. When released, we were ordered into the admiral's tender, which was to convey us to the Nore. Here we were called over by name, nearly two hundred, including a number of the Lord Mayor's Men, a term given to those who enter to relieve themselves from public disgrace, and who are sent on board by any of the city magistrates, for a street frolic or night charge. These poor fellows have a sad time of it, as they are the derision of the old and more experienced and hardened sailors, who generally cut the tails from their coats, and otherwise abuse and ridicule them. Upon getting on board this vessel, we were ordered down in the hold, and the gratings put over us; as well as a guard of marines placed round the hatch way, with their muskets loaded and fixed bayonets, as though we had been culprits of the first degree, or capital convicts. In this place we spent the day and following night huddled together, for there was not room to sit or stand separate: indeed, we were in a pitiable plight, for numbers of them were seasick, some retching, others were smoking, whilst many were so overcome by the stench, that they fainted for want of air. As soon as the officer on deck understood that the men below were overcome with foul air, he ordered the hatches to be taken off, when daylight broke in upon us; and a wretched appearance we cut, for scarcely any of us were free from filth and vermin. We had by this time arrived at the Nore, and were all ordered on deck, where boats from the receiving ships were alongside to take us away from the tender, and place us on board those ships, where we were supplied with slops, the price of which is stopt from our pay by the purser, and in due time we were transferred and distributed among the different ships, where we awaited an order for a supply of men and boys, to complete each ship's complement. I must here state a regular system of plunder observed on hoard of those ships, on the birds of passage, as we were called, more than was agreeable, partly perhaps, from what may now he termed larking, but principally from a wicked design. Some lost their shoes in the open day, while others had their blankets taken from them as they lay on the deck at night; they would disappear instantaneously, as if by magic. The mode resorted to, I learned, was by using fishhooks and a line, which were contrived so dextrously, that, aided by its being dark between decks, it was almost impossible to detect them.

From this ship I was drafted on board a line of battleship, then fitting out to join Lord Nelson. Whilst lying here, two of our men got down by the head of the ship into the water, tying their clothes round their necks. One of them got clear off; the other stuck in the mud, and being nearly exhausted, he called out for assistance. It being dark at the time, one of our boats rowed in the direction the voice came from; and there, one of our men stuck so fast in the mud, that it required two of the boat's crew to pull him out.

We were now fast getting our ship ready for sea, and in a few days sailed past the Downs to Portsmouth, and joined the Channel fleet. Here we began to feel discipline with all its horrors. Our crew was divided into two watches, starboard and larboard. When one was on deck the other was below: for instance, the starboard watch would come on at eight o'clock at night, which is called eight-bells; at half-past is called one bell, and so on; every half-hour is a bell, as the hourglass is turned, and the messenger sent to strike the bell, which is generally affixed near the fore-hatchway. It now becomes the duty of the officer on deck to see that the logline is run out, to ascertain how many knots the ship goes an hour, which is entered in the logbook, with any other occurrence which may take place during the watch.

At twelve o'clock, or eight-bells in the first watch, the boatswain's mate calls out lustily, "Larboard watch, a-hoy." This is called the middle watch, and when on deck, the other watch go below to their hammocks, till eight-bells, which is four o'clock in the morning. They then come on deck again, pull off their shoes and stockings, turn up their trousers to above their knees, and commence holy-stoning the deck, as it is termed, (for Jack is sometimes a little impious in the way of his sayings.)—Here the men suffer from being obliged to kneel down on the wetted deck, and a gravelly sort of sand strewed over it. To perform this work they kneel with their bare knees, rubbing the deck with a stone and the sand, the grit of which is often very injurious. In this manner the watch continues till about four-bells, or six o'clock; they then begin to wash and swab the decks till seven bells, and at eight-bells the boatswain's mate pipes to breakfast. This meal usually consists of burgoo, made of coarse oatmeal and water; others will have Scotch coffee, which is burnt bread boiled in some water, and sweetened with sugar. This is generally cooked in a hook-pot in the galley, where there is a range. Nearly all the crew have one of these pots, a spoon, and a knife; for these are things indispensable: there are also basons, plates, &c. which are kept in each mess, which generally consists of eight persons, whose berth is between two of the guns on the lower deck, where there is a board placed, which swings with the rolling of the ship, and answers for a table.

It sometimes happens that a lurch will dash all the crockery to pieces; they are then obliged to eat out of wooden or tin utensils, until they come into harbour, where they get another supply. At half-past eight o'clock, or one-bell in the fore-noon watch, the larboard goes on deck and the starboard remains below. Here again the holy-stones or hand-bibles as they are called by the crew, are used, and sometimes iron scrapers. After the lower deck has been wetted with swabs, these scrapers are used to take the rough dirt off. Whilst this is going on, the cooks from each mess are employed in cleaning the utensils and preparing for dinner, at the same time the watch are working the ship, and doing what is wanting to be done on deck.

About eleven o'clock, or six bells, when any of the men are in irons, or on the black list, the boatswain or mate are ordered to call all hands; the culprits are then brought forward by the master at arms, who is a warrant officer, and acts the part of Jack Ketch, when required: he likewise has the prisoners in his custody, until they are put in irons, under any charge.

All hands being now mustered, the captain orders the man to strip; he is then seized to a grating by the wrists and knees; his crime is then mentioned, and the prisoner may plead, but, in nineteen cases out of twenty, he is flogged for the most trifling offence or neglect, such as not hearing the watch called at night, not doing any thing properly on deck or aloft, which he might happen to be sent to do, when, perhaps he has been doing the best he could, and at the same time ignorant of having done wrong, until he is pounced on, and put in irons. So much for the legal process.

After punishment, the boatswain's mate pipes to

dinner, it being eight-bells, or twelve o'clock; and this is the pleasantest part of the day, as at one bell the fifer is called to play "Nancy Dawson," or some other lively tune, a well-known signal that the grog is ready to be served out. It is the duty of the cook from each mess to fetch and serve it out to his messmates, of which every man and boy is allowed a pint, that is, one gill of rum and three of water, to which is added lemon acid, sweetened with sugar.

Here I must remark, that the cook comes in for the perquisites of office, by reserving to himself an extra portion of grog, which is called the overplus, and generally comes to the double of a man's allowance. Thus the cook can take upon himself to be the man of consequence, for he has the opportunity of inviting a friend to partake of a glass, or of paying any little debt he may have contracted. It may not be known to every one that it is grog, which pays debts, and not money, in a man of war.

Notwithstanding the cook's apparently pre-eminent situation, yet, on some occasions, he is subject to censure or punishment by his messmates, for not attending to the dinner properly, or suffering the utensils of his department to be in a dirty condition. Justice, in these cases, is awarded by packing a jury of cooks from the different messes, for it falls to the lot of each man in a mess to act as cook in his turn. The mode or precept by which this jury is summoned is by hoisting a mess swab or beating a tin dish between decks forward, which serves as a proclamation to call the court together, when the case is fully heard and decided upon.

At two-bells in the afternoon, or one o'clock, the starboard watch goes on deck, and remains working the ship, pointing the ropes, or doing any duty that may be required until the eight-bells strike, when the boatswain's mate pipes to supper. This consists of half a pint of wine, or a pint of grog to each man, with biscuit and cheese, or butter.

At the one bell, or half-past four, which is called one bell in the first dogwatch, the larboard watch comes on duty, and remains until six o'clock, when that is relieved by the starboard watch, which is called the second dogwatch, which lasts till eight o'clock. To explain this, it must be observed that these four hours, from four to eight o'clock, are divided into two watches, with a view of making the other watches come regular and alternate, and are called the first and second dog-watch. By this regular system of duty, I became inured to the roughness and hardships of a sailor's life. I had made up my mind to be obedient, however irksome to my feelings, and our ship being on the Channel station, I soon began to pick up a knowledge of seamanship.

After beating about the Channel for some time, we were ordered to proceed along the Spanish coast, to look after the combined fleets of France and Spain. Having heard that Sir Robert Calder had fallen in with them a few days previous, we pursued our course, looking in at Ferrol and other ports, until we arrived off Cadiz, where we found they had got safe in. Here we continued to blockade them, until Lord Nelson joined us with five sail of the line.

In order to decoy the enemy out, stratagem was resorted to, and five sail were sent to Gibraltar to victual and water, whilst Lord Nelson, with his five sail, kept out of sight of the enemy, and thus they thought we were only twenty two sail of the line, whilst their fleet consisted of thirty-three sail. With this superior force they put to sea, with the intention, as we afterwards learned, of taking our fleet; and, if they had succeeded, possessed of so great a force, they were to occupy the Channel, and assist in the invasion of England by the troops then encamped along the French coast, with an immense number of flat-bottomed boats, with which the French ports swarmed; but here, as in many other instances, they reckoned without their host. British valour and seamanship frustrated their design, and destroyed their hopes; for on the memorable 21st of October, 1805, as the day began to dawn, a man at the topmast head called out, "a sail on the starboard bow," and in two or three minutes more he gave another call, that there was more than one sail, for indeed they looked like a forest of masts rising from the ocean; and, as the morning got light, we could plainly discern them from the deck, and were satisfied it was the enemy, for the admiral began to telegraph to that effect. They saw us, and would gladly have got away when they discovered that we counted twenty-seven sail of the line, but it was too late, situated as they were; hemmed in by Cape Trafalgar on the one side, and not being able to get back to Cadiz on the other.

As the enemy was thus driven to risk a battle, they exhibited a specimen of their naval tactics by forming themselves into a crescent, or half-moon, waiting for our approach; which did not take place until ten minutes of twelve o'clock, so that there was nearly six hours to prepare for battle; while we glided down to them under the influence of a gentle breeze, cheering to every seaman's heart, that Providence took us in tow; and from a signal made by Lord Nelson, our ships were soon formed into two lines, weather and lee.

Jack's ship, the 74-gun ship-of-the-line, *Revenge*

(Artist T. Robinson)

Preparing for Battle

During this time each ship was making the usual preparations, such as breaking away the captain and officer's cabins, and sending all the lumber below—the doctors, parson, purser and loblolly men, were also busy, getting the medicine chests and bandages out; and sails prepared for the wounded to be placed on, that they might be dressed in rotation, as they were taken down to the after cock-pit. In such a bustling, and it may be said, trying as well as serious time, it is curious to notice the different dispositions of the British sailor. Some would be offering a guinea for a glass of grog, whilst others were making a sort of mutual verbal will, such as, if one of Johnny Crapeau's shots, (a term given to the French,) knocks my head off, you will take all my effects; and if you are killed, and I am not, why, I will have yours, and this is generally agreed to. During this momentous preparation, the human mind had ample time for meditation and conjecture, for it was evident that the fate of England rested on this battle; therefore well might Lord Nelson make the signal, "England expects each man will do his duty."

Here, if I may be indulged the observation, I will say that, could England but have seen her sons about to attack the enemy on his own coast, within sight of the inhabitants of Spain, with an inferior force, our number of men being not quite twenty thousand, whilst theirs was upwards of thirty thousand; from the zeal which animated every man in the fleet, the bosom of every inhabitant of England would have glowed with an indescribable patriotic pride; for such a number of line-of-battle ships have never met together and engaged, either before or since. As we drew near, we discovered the enemy's line was formed with a Spanish ship between two French ones, nearly all through their line; as I suppose, to make them fight better; and it must be admitted that the Dons fought as well as the French in that battle; and, if praise was due for seamanship and valour, they were well entitled to an equal share. We now began to hear the enemy's cannon opening on the Royal Sovereign, commanded by Lord Collingwood, who commenced the action; and, a signal being made by the admiral to some of our senior captains to break the enemy's line at different points, it fell to our lot to cut off the five sternmost ships; and, while we were running down to them, of course we were favoured with several shots, and some of our men were wounded. Upon being thus pressed, many of our men thought it hard that the firing should be all on one side, and became impatient to return the compliment: but our captain had given orders not to fire until we got close in with them, so that all our shot might tell;—indeed, these were his words: "We shall want all our shot when we get close in: never mind their firing: when I fire a carronade from the quarter-deck, that will be a signal for you to begin, and I know you will do your duty as Englishmen." In a few minutes the gun was fired, and our ship bore in and broke the line, but we paid dear for our temerity, as those ships we had thrown into disorder turned round, and made an attempt to board. A Spanish three-decker ran her bowsprit over our poop, with a number of her crew on it, and, in her fore rigging, two or three hundred men were ready to follow; but they caught a Tartar, for their design was discovered, and our marines with their small arms, and the carronades on the poop, loaded with canister shot, swept them off so fast, some into the water, and some on the decks, that they were glad to sheer off. While this was going on aft, we were engaged with a French two-deck ship on our starboard side, and on our larboard bow another, so that many of their shots must have struck their own ships, and done severe execution. After being engaged about an hour, two other ships fortunately came up, received some of the fire intended for us, and we were now enabled to get at some of the shot-holes between wind and water, and plug them up:—this is a duty performed by the carpenter and his crew. We were now unable to work the ship, our yards, sails, and masts being disabled, and the braces completely shot away. In this condition we lay by the side of the enemy, firing away, and now and then we received a good raking from them, passing under our stern. This was a busy time with us, for we had not only to endeavour to repair our damage, but to keep to our duty. Often during the battle we could not see for the smoke, whether we were firing at a foe or friend, and as to hearing, the noise of the guns had so completely made us deaf, that we were obliged to look only to the motions that were made. In this manner we continued the battle till near five o'clock, when it ceased.

It was shortly after made known by one of our boat's crew, that Lord Nelson had received a fatal shot: had this news been communicated through the fleet before the conflict was over, what effect it might have had on the hearts of our seamen I know not, for he was adored, and in fighting under him, every man thought himself sure of success; a momentary but naturally melancholy pause among the survivors of our brave crew ensued.

We were now called to clear the decks, and here might be witnessed an awful and interesting scene, for as each officer and seaman would meet, (oh! what an opportunity for the Christian and man of feeling to meditate on the casualty of fate in this life,) they were inquiring for their messmates. Orders were now given to fetch the dead bodies from the after cock-pit, and throw them over-board; these were the bodies of men who were taken down to the doctor during the battle, badly wounded, and who by the time the engagement was ended were dead. Some of these, perhaps, could not have recovered, while others might, had timely assistance been rendered, which was impossible; for the rule is, as order is requisite, that every person shall be dressed in rotation as they are brought down wounded, and in many instances some have bled to death.

The next call was, "all hands to splice the main brace," which is the giving out a gill of rum to each man, and indeed they much needed it, for they had not ate or drank from breakfast time: we had now a good night's work before us; all our yards, masts, and sails were sadly cut, indeed the whole of the sails were obliged to be unbent, being rendered completely useless, and by the next morning we were partly jury-rigged: we now began to look for our prizes, as it was coming on to blow hard on the land, and Admiral Collingwood made signals for each ship that was able, to take a prize in tow, to prevent them drifting into their own harbour, as they were complete wrecks and unmanageable.

We took an eighty gun Spanish ship in tow for a day and night, but were obliged to cast her off, it blew so hard, and our ship being so very much disabled, indeed we were obliged to scuttle a few of them; some we contrived to take into Gibraltar; some were wrecked near Cadiz harbour; and others drifted into the harbour from whence they had only come out two days before. It was a mortifying sight to witness the ships we had fought so hard for, and had taken as prizes, driven by the elements from our possession, with some of our own men on board as prize masters, and it was a great blight to our victorious success; but, in justice to the enemy, it may with truth be recorded, that, however contrary to the Spanish character as an enemy generally, yet, upon this occasion, they used our men well.

In order to show the crippled state in which our ships must have been, it will be requisite to mention that, in preparing to engage the enemy closely, and protect ourselves as much as possible, the seamen's hammocks with the bedding and blanket were lashed to the shrouds, which served much to save our rigging, as was very evident from examination on the second night after the battle; for when our men got their hammocks down, many were found to have received a great deal of damage, being very much cut with the large shot, and some were found to have had grape or canister shot lodged in them. The most destructive shot to us appeared to be the thirty-two pounds double-headed; two of these deafeners we observed to be sticking in our main-mast, which, miraculously and fortunately for us, was not carried away.

I will now call the reader's attention to some occurrences during and after the battle, which, although they may not regularly belong to a seaman's log, yet they may be found interesting.

The advantage of learning to dance

As we were closely engaged throughout the battle, and the shots were playing their pranks pretty freely, grape as well as canister, with single and double headed thunderers all joining in the frolic; what was termed a *slaughtering one*, came in at one of the lower deck ports, which killed and wounded nearly all at the gun, and amongst them, a very merry little fellow, who was the very life of the ship's company, for he was ever the mirth of his mess, and on whatever duty he might be ordered, his spirits made light the labour. He was the ship's cobbler, and withall a very good dancer; so that when any of his messmates would *sarve* us out a tune, he was sure to trip it on light fantastic toe, and find a step to it. He happened to be stationed at the gun where this messenger of death and destruction entered, and the poor fellow was so completely stunned by the head of another man being knocked against his, that no one doubted but that he was dead.

As it is customary to throw overboard those, who, in an engagement are killed outright, the poor cobbler, amongst the rest, was taken to the port-hole to be committed to the deep, without any other ceremony than shoving him through the port: but, just as they were about to let him slip from their hands into the water, the blood began to circulate, and he commenced kicking. Upon this sign of returning life, his shipmates soon hauled the poor snob in again, and, though wonderful to relate, he recovered so speedily, that he actually fought the battle out; and, when he was afterwards joked about it, he would say, "it was well that I learned to dance: for if I had not shown you some of my steps, when you were about to throw me overboard, I should not be here now, but safe enough in *Davy Jones's Locker.*"

The danger of giving too much power into the hands of young officers

If an officer is of a tyrannical disposition on board a ship, whatever accident may happen to him, he will never receive pity or commiseration from any of the ship's crew; as, for instance, we had a midshipman on board our ship of a wickedly mischievous disposition, whose sole delight was to insult the feelings of the seamen, and furnish pretexts to get them punished. His conduct made every man's life miserable that happened to be under his orders. He was a youth not more than twelve or thirteen years of age; but I have often seen him get on the carriage of a gun, call a man to him, and kick him about the thighs and body, and with his fist would beat him about the head; and these, although prime seamen, at the same time dared not murmur. It was ordained however, by Providence, that his reign of terror and severity should not last; for during the engagement, he was killed on the quarter-deck by a grape-shot, his body greatly mutilated, his entrails being driven and scattered against the larboard side; nor were there any lamentations for his fate!—No! for when it was known that he was killed, the general exclamation was? *"Thank God, we are rid of the young tyrant!"* His death was hailed as the triumph over an enemy.

Conjugal affection and heroinism of a French Female

Whilst we were engaging the combined fleets, a French ship caught fire, the crew of which made every effort to escape from the flames, and as *"Britons fight but to conquer, and conquer to save,"* our frigates and schooners, which had been laying off during the battle, sent their boats to endeavour to save as many lives as possible. Amongst those who were thus preserved from a watery grave was a young French woman, who was brought on board our ship in a slate of complete nakedness Although it was in the heat of the battle, yet she received every assistance which at that time was in our power; and her distress of mind was soothed as well as we could, until the officers got to their chests, from whence they supplied her with needles and thread, to convert sheets into chemises, and curtains from their cots to make somewhat of a gown, and other garments, so that by degrees she was made as comfortable as circumstances would admit; for we all tried who would be most kind to her; and as the history of this adventurer may acquire some interest from the account she gave of it, the following is the statement, as collected from herself;—

The combined fleets, (she says) were ordered to proceed from Cadiz, where they lay, to make an attack and take that of the British; for, from their superior force they were confident of success, and elated at the same time with the idea that it would be but an easy task. That no impediment might be in the way, all the females were ordered to go on shore; she was married, and to quit her husband could not endure the thought; she was therefore resolved to share his glory or his death. No time was lost in carrying her plan into execution; for, having rigged herself out in a suit of sailor's clothes, thus disguised, she entered on board, and went in the same ship with him, as a seaman. In this state she remained, doing duty, during the engagement, when, whilst fighting by the side of her husband, a ball killed him on the spot. On seeing him fall dead, the conflict was too great:— nature displayed itself; she became overwhelmed with grief, and, by it, betrayed her sex.

To add to the distress which this discovery occasioned, an alarm was now spread that the ship was on fire; she seemed to care very little about it; life to her was not desirable, whilst all hands were employed in the endeavour to check the fire's progress. This seemed to be impossible, and it became necessary to think of the means to escape; for the fire raged with great fury, and there was every probability that, in a few minutes, the ship would be blown into the air, as the fire was fast approaching the magazines.

The resolution to take to the water being now unavoidable, the men commenced to undress themselves; and in this dreadful situation she was strongly urged to do the same, that "it was a duty to make every effort for self-preservation, and it being the only chance she could possibly have. After much entreaty, persuasion, and remonstrance, she summoned up sufficient resolution, and prepared herself to endure the agonizing alternative, for the only choice, which her unfortunate case presented, was, either to strip, or perish in the flames. She was then lowered into the ocean by a rope from the taffrail, the lead of which was melting at the lime, and, whilst letting her down, some of it dropped, and burned the back of her neck. On reaching the water, one of her shipmates, who was a good swimmer, staid by her side, and supported her until she was picked up by a boat belonging to the Fickle schooner, and brought on board the ship she was then in." [Here let the reader pause, and paint to himself, if he can, what were the inward workings and heartfelt sufferings of this extraordinary heroine, and bright instance of conjugal fidelity and attachment.]

Her name was Jeannette, of French Flanders, and she remained with us until our arrival at Gibraltar, when a cartel took her to a Spanish port. On leaving our ship, her heart seemed overwhelmed with gratitude; she shed abundance of tears, and could only now and then, with a deep sigh, exclaim, *"les bom Anglois."*

The Day after the Battle

Some of our men were sent on board of the Spanish ship before alluded to, in order to assist at the pumps, for she was much shattered in the hull, between wind and water. The slaughter and havoc our guns had made, rendered the scene of carnage horrid to behold: there were a number of their dead bodies piled up in the hold; many, in a wounded or mutilated state, were found lying amongst them; and those who were so fortunate as to escape our shot, were so dejected and crestfallen, that they could not, or would not, work at the pumps, and of course the ship was in a sinking state.

The gale at this time was increasing so rapidly, that manning the pumps was of no use, and we were obliged to abandon our prize, taking away with us all our men, and as many of the prisoners as we could. On the last boat's load leaving the ship, the Spaniards who were left on board, appeared on the gangway and ship's side, displaying their bags of dollars and doubloons, and eagerly offering them as a reward for saving them from the expected and unavoidable wreck; but, however well inclined we were, it was not in our power to rescue them, or it would have been effected without the proffered bribe.

Here a very distressing and affecting scene took place; it was a struggle between inclination and duty. On quitting the ship, our boats were overloaded in endeavouring to save all the lives we could, that it is a miracle they were not upset. A father and his son came down the ship's side to get on board one of our boats; the father had seated himself, but the men in the boat, thinking, from the load and the boisterous weather, that all their lives would be in peril, could not think of taking the boy; as the boat put off, the lad, as though determined not to quit his father, sprung from the ship into the water, and caught hold of the gunwale of the boat; but his attempt was resisted, as it risked all their lives, and some of the men resorted to their cutlasses to cut his fingers off, in order to disentangle the boat from his grasp; at the same time the feelings of the father were so worked upon, that he was about to leap overboard, and perish with his son: Britons could face an enemy, but could not witness such a scene of self-devotion; as it were, a simultaneous thought burst forth from the crew, which said "let us save both father and son, or die in the attempt." The Almighty aided them in their design; they succeeded, and brought both father and son safe on board of our ship, where they remained, until, with other prisoners, they were exchanged at Gibraltar.

Arrival at Gibraltar

Whilst we were at this place, patching our shattered hulls, to make us sea-worthy for returning home; some of the crews belonging to the different ships in the fleet would occasionally meet on shore and one would say to another tauntingly, on enquiring to what ship he belonged; "oh! you belong to one of the ships that did not come up till the battle was nearly over;" and others would be heard to say, "oh! you belong to one of the Boxing Twelves, come and have some black strap and Malaga wine," at the same time giving them a hearty shake by the hand. This was signifying that the heat of the battle was borne by the twelve ships which first engaged and broke the line; and though in a great measure this was true; yet no fault or blame could be attributed either to the officers or men belonging to those ships, as it was the tremendous firing from the ships first engaged, which so becalmed the waters and lulled the winds, that a few of our largest ships could only come up in time to receive a straggling shot or two, and take possession of some of the prizes.

There are not many persons, perhaps, who would believe that the firing of cannon could have such an effect on the air and the waters; but a little reflection will convince of its truth, when they learn the notorious fact, that one gun will have power to burst a raging water-spout; and then it may be imagined what effect must be produced from a thousand cannons, heavily charged, every minute, for some hours.

Safe arrival at Home

Our ship being made sea-worthy, we set sail for Old England, and arrived safe at Spithead. The next day we weighed anchor for Portsmouth; and, on our way into the harbour-mouth, we were loudly cheered, and welcomed home by an immense number of persons, who came out to greet us on the occasion. The ship being put into dock to repair, the crew were sent on board of a hulk, from which many of them obtained a temporary leave of absence, and, among the rest, I had a six days liberty ticket, with which, and two shillings and nine-pence in my pocket, I was resolved to go to London; I landed at Gosport, and proceeded on my road to the boundary of the town, where the soldiers stopt me; but, after showing them my liberty ticket, and having a little parley with them, I was allowed to go on. I bent my course forward until I reached Fareham, and being aware that a pressgang was lurking about that neighbourhood, I felt very much inclined to give them a little trouble: I had gone nearly through the town unobserved by them; but at length the alarm was given, that a sailor was making good his way in full sail towards

London; when two members of that worthless set of body snatchers set out in pursuit. I could, by keeping a good look-out, observe their movements, and I walked sharply on; they commenced running, I did the same, and kept well on until I arrived at an inn by the road-side, where I thought proper to stop, and let them come up with me; I did not take any notice of them, nor show any appearance of alarm; but, supposing I was a prize, one of them grappled me on the starboard, and the other on the larboard side, by the collar of my jacket, demanding the name of the ship I belonged to; when on coolly showing them my liberty ticket, they showered a broadside of curses on me for giving them such a run, and quietly left me to pursue my journey. After this however, I had to contend with the landsharks; for, on my arrival at Alton, I was stopped by a party of soldiers, to whose inspection I had again to exhibit my ticket of leave; and thus, for thirty miles from the sea-port, was a poor seaman hunted by this detestable set, who are constantly watching, in the bye lanes and fields, to intercept any seaman who may be passing that way; the inducement held out to these men stealers is five pounds for each seaman they may capture; and thus many a poor fellow is hunted by those bloodhounds, who chase them with greater eagerness than the huntsman pursues the fox. After getting so far clear of those nests of vipers, I proceeded on to London, where I stayed with my friends until my liberty was out.

On returning to Portsmouth, I learned that our captain had left, and that another had taken the command; I also found that a vast number of our men had run, in consequence of our new captain having the character of being a tyrannical officer. This self-important nautical demagogue very soon set about, not a reform, but a revolution in the ship. It had been a favorite mode with Lord Nelson to paint the sides of all the ships under his command in chequers, which made them to be distinguished with greater certainty in case of falling in with an enemy; and became a well known and general term in a squadron or fleet, so much so that, when speaking of any other ship, it was usual to say, "oh! she's one of Nelson's chequer-players," signifying thereby that she had been one of the fighting ships. The seamen liked the distinction, and took great pride in being considered as a chequer-player, and could not wish to part with the name; but no sooner had this self-sufficient blusterer come on board, and possessed himself of the reins of government, than he changed the painting of the ship's side from that of a chequer to a single stripe.

The character which came on board with him was quite sufficient to create dissatisfaction in the ship's company, but this single act caused so much disgust, that nothing was heard but execrations on his head; for it seemed as though he had studiously intended to blot out or rob them of what they considered as the badge of their glory. "Ah," many might be heard to say, "that fellow never liked the smell of powder, I'm sure, for it's a d—d cowardly act; and the greater the tyrant, the greater the coward: and if the signal was made now for him to advance and engage an enemy, he'd lag a-stern: no, he'll never be a chequer-player, let him command for fifty years to come." This worthy, whose name was a terror to every ship's company he commanded, and was cursed from stem to stern in the British navy, now shines forth as an M. P. and is always to be found at his post; and whenever the subjects of impressment or flogging in the navy or army is brought forward in the House of Commons, he is ever ready with his Nero heart, and famed for his skill in the support of these diabolical systems.

Blockade of Sourdeaux and Rochefort

It happened, very fortunately for us, that this honorable gentleman did not go out with ns: the cause of the change I know not; but, at all events, we were joined by another captain, who, to our great rejoicing, Nelsonified us again, by painting our ship chequer-sided, and so took us to sea.

In a short time we found ourselves hovering about and blockading Bourdeaux and Rochefort; and we soon commenced operations against some shipping lying in the former place. There were a number of merchantmen waiting for an opportunity to get out to sea, under the protection of two French gun-brigs: our commodore made signals for each ship to prepare a large boat or launch, to endeavour to cut them out in the night. Some of our best men, to the amount of twenty, volunteered in a large pinnace, with muffled oars, commanded by a lieutenant, and accompanied by a midshipman, who with the boats and launches from the other ships, entered Bourdeaux harbour; but were soon discovered by the enemy, who began to play the shot from their batteries pretty smartly: one of them struck our boat; killed the lieutenant and one of the men, and likewise sunk the boat, and the remainder of her crew were picked up by the French and made prisoners, when no assistance could be rendered them by us, the boats from the other ships being too much occupied in boarding the gun-brigs, one of which they captured, and the other they were obliged to abandon, as the shot from the batteries was so terrific.

Engagement with a French Squadron

Soon after we had recovered ourselves from this little encounter, we got entangled with another; for five French frigates, with two hundred and fifty seamen and five hundred troops on board of each ship, destined to relieve one of their West India islands, came out from Rochefort in the evening, when it became dark, think to evade us during the night. Their commodore made a signal with lanterns to "bout ship,' and it was somewhat singular that this signal happened to be our signal for "an enemy." They soon found we were in pursuit of them, and made all sail to get away; they were frigates of 44 guns each, and sailed well. After a hard chase, a part of our squadron got within gun-shot of one, then another was brought to action, and so on, until we had taken four, and the fifth probably would have belonged to us, had the captain of a line-of-battle ship been allowed to engage her. This ship's signal was made to make all sail to assist the commodore, who had his arm shot off; and as his ship was a seventy-four, and was only engaged by a 44 gun frigate, we were at a loss to know what assistance he wanted.

After they had struck, about sixty of our ship's crew were sent on board, to take possession of one of them, and I am compelled to say, that, like most Englishmen, they began to think of number one, and look after what good things might be grappled; and the work of destruction began by boarding the stock of fresh provisions, Cognac brandy, and wine, of all which our prize had a profusion. Some of the men filled cabbage-nets with eggs, and some put them into the copper to boil, others got a sheep, killed it, took the skin, and head off, and put that too in the copper, without taking the trouble to disjoint it, for that was a ceremony dispensed with; and in this manner the greater part of our men were pleasantly engaged, preparing for a fresh meal, which to them was a luxury, as they had been living for some time previous on salt provisions. Some were obliged to attend below to hurry the prisoners on deck, as our boats were in waiting alongside to take them away. Here the cries of the wounded were really heart-rending; and, to make the scene the more distressing, the French doctor having lost or mislaid some of his instruments, he was reduced to the necessity of resorting to the use of the carpenter's fine saw, where amputation was needful: and after securing our prizes, they were sent home to Plymouth.

Our ships still continued the blockade, until they were separated by a tremendous gale of wind, which lasted for several days; and we were completely at the mercy of each succeeding mountainous dashing wave, for we were not able to show a stitch of canvas; in this perilous situation we were, when, on a sudden, at about three-bells in the middle-watch, the Mars, a 74 gun ship, appeared on the top of a wave, while our ship was in the valley beneath, and it was thought by all on board, that we must inevitably come into contact, strike each other, and go down. The presence of mind of a seam, in this moment of danger, was happily displayed by his grasping of the storm-staysail-halliards, and with assistance the sail was hoisted, so that the ship's head was turned, by which means we cleared her; the next minute the sail flew to pieces, and resembled the smacking of so many whips, and the succeeding wave separated us.

We saw each other no more during the gale, which abated two days after; and as we were close to the French coast, we ran into Quiberon bay, where the Pickle schooner joined us, she was in the gale, and had the whole of the watch on deck swept away, by one of those mountainous waves breaking over her. Having repaired our damage, we put to sea, and joined our squadron; from which we were soon after ordered home to England.

On arriving at Spithead, we found it had been reported that our ship was lost, the Mars having seen us in such a perilous situation; and having lost sight of us in a moment naturally thought that we were ingulphed in the trough of the enormous waves which passed between us.

Joining the Blockade off Cadiz

After refitting, we sailed to join the blockading squadron, off Cadiz, and remained there about eighteen months, during which time we were tacking or wearing ship continually, as the blockading service required us to keep as near the harbour's mouth as possible, and consequently, when the wind was blowing on the land, we were obliged to beat off; and when it was blowing off the land, then to beat up to the harbour's mouth as near as we could, to prevent the escape of the enemy. Whilst on this station, we sometimes fired at, and brought to, some of the Spanish fishing-boats, and by these means, a fresh meal for the crew was of ten obtained; for they not only had fish on board, but some would have grapes, whilst others would have fowls and eggs; and our captain was always anxious to get fresh provision for the ship's company.

Whilst on the look-out, we happened to discover the enemy one morning loose their sails, and this we thought was merely to dry them, but it turned out to be otherwise. A Russian fleet, of nine sail of the line, had just come down the Gut of Gibraltar, and wanted to enter Cadiz harbour; we were now in rather an awkward predicament, not being certain whether that nation had declared war with England or not; but at all events we prepared for action.

Our admiral sent his boat, with an officer, to the Russian admiral, to inform him that he could not go in, and, if he attempted, that we must dispute the point with him. Our force being nine sail of the line, made us but equal, yet we were in an awkward position, for on the other side of us were ten or eleven sail of French and Spanish ships of the line, ready to come out, and no doubt would give their assistance to cripple us. The Russians, however, shaped their course to Lisbon; and where I believe they were afterwards captured by one of our squadrons.

Whilst hovering about here, we often had spies, under various pretences, coming to us from the shore. The small-arms men and marines were daily exercised on board of the different ships, with orders to hold themselves in readiness to land and storm the batteries. Anxious for this frolic, we were all preparation, when a boat was seen making all sail towards us, with a flag of truce, bringing favors from Ferdinand VII.

It appeared, from the statement they made, that the governor of Cadiz was in league with Bonaparte, and was on the point of giving the town up to the French, whose messenger had been intercepted, his papers examined, and were found to contain the stipulations between the governor and Bonaparte; when this had got wind, it soon became generally known: the governor was seized and beheaded; and his head was carried about on a pole. Some of the incensed mob showed revenge by getting a cut at the lifeless trunk; and if he could carry away a piece of the flesh as a trophy, he would be highly gratified. They applied to us for assistance against the French, who were about to entrap them by their secret workings: and, as British sailors scorn deception and false play, from being rank enemies, we became friends.

It turned out that they much wanted our aid, for on going to the magazine, it was found that the governor had caused the powder to be removed on board the French ships of war, and had deceitfully placed sand in its stead; but, fortunately for them, our ships could supply them with powder.

We anchored at the mouth of the harbour, where we lay about a week; and, during that time, the Spaniards were throwing shot and shells at the French fleet. After summoning them to surrender, which they did not notice until the furnace with hot shot was ready to play on them; and being informed that no quarters would be given, and the time allowed for their final answer; after repeated flags of truce having arrived, the French admiral surrendered, with five or six ships of the line.

Now the Spaniards wanted greater immediate assistance than we could afford them, and our ship was ordered to England with two of the Spanish chiefs upon business with our government. When about to leave Cadiz, a boat came off with a friar to us, whom we brought to England, as he deemed it prudent to quit, in consequence of the French troops having demolished and ransacked the monasteries and convents. A vast number of the inmates of the religious houses were obliged to fly, and take refuge on board of the British ships, and were afterwards sent to their own colonies in South Spanish America.

Our passage to old England was long and tedious, as the wind was foul nearly all the way, and beating is heart-breaking to sailors. It was a time of painful anxiety to all on board, for what could be more tormenting than to be homeward-bound, hearts panting with the anticipated happiness of meeting wives and sweethearts, or other relatives and friends, and a lubberly head-wind playing with your distress: can anything more distressing be imagined? But a sailor's mind is not to be overcome by accidents or disappointments; he meets them as he would an enemy, by facing them, and merrily sings, "grieving's a folly, boys!" Every plan is resorted to, to keep up the spirits, and nautical wit on these occasions generally displays itself.

A head-wind is the constant topic, and the boatswain, on coming upon deck, would look about him, to see how the wind was, and, with a great deal of good humour and apparent seriousness, would swear most positively that we should never have a fair wind whilst that holy friar was on board; and all the bad luck on board was set down to his account; others might be heard to say, that their wives and lasses had not got hold of the tow-rope; a phrase intimating that, from being absent so long, they had taken to themselves other husbands in harbour, and did not want them home yet; with many other forecastle pleasantries to drive away melancholy.

In England once again

On our arrival at Spithead, when the Spanish chiefs were about to leave the ship, we fired a salute, and, on the smoke clearing away, they could observe that our yards were manned, and the ship dressed in colours, with which they appeared to be thankfully pleased. Report said, that so urgent did their cause appear to our government, that Sir John Moore was immediately sent out with an army, but from which he unfortunately never returned to relate the result.

After having moored our ship, swarms of boats came round us; some were what are generally termed bomb-boats, but are really nothing but floating chandler's shops; and a great many of them were freighted with cargoes of ladies, a sight that was truly gratifying, and a great treat; for our crew, consisting of six hundred and upwards, nearly all young men, had seen but one woman on board for eighteen months, and that was the daughter of one of the Spanish chiefs, who made no stay on board, but went on shore again immediately.

So soon as these boats were allowed to come alongside, the seamen flocked down pretty quick, one after the other, and brought their choice up, so that in the course of the afternoon, we had about four hundred and fifty on board.

Of all the human race, these poor young creatures are the most pitiable; the ill-usage and the degradation they are driven to submit to, are indescribable; but from habit they become callous, indifferent as to delicacy of speech and behaviour, and so totally lost to all sense of shame, that they seem to retain no quality which properly belongs to woman, but the shape and name. When we reflect that these unfortunately deluded victims to our passions, might at one time have been destined to be the valuable companions and comforts of man, but now so fallen: in these cooler moments of meditation, what a charge is raised against ourselves; we cannot reproach them for their abject condition, lest this startling question should be asked of us, who made us so?

On the arrival of any man of war in port, these girls flock down to the shore, where boats are always ready; and here may be witnessed a scene, somewhat similar to the trafficking for slaves in the West Indies. As they approached a boat, old Charon, with painter in hand, before they step on board, surveys them from stem to stern, with the eyes of a bargaining jew; and carefully culls out the best looking, and the most dashingly dressed; and, in making up his complement for a load, it often happens that he refuses to take some of them, observing, (very politely) and usually with some vulgar oath; to one, that she is too old; to another, that "she is too ugly; and that he shall not be able to sell them; and he'll be d—d if he has any notion of having his trouble for nothing.

The only apology that can be made for the savage conduct of these unfeeling brutes is, that they run a chance of not being permitted to carry a cargo alongside, unless it makes a good show-off; for it has been often known, that, on approaching a ship, the officer in command has so far forgot himself as to order the waterman to push off—that he should not bring such a cargo of d—d ugly devils on board, and that he would not allow any of his men to have them. At this ungentlemanly rebuff, the waterman lays upon his oars a-while, hangs his lip, musing on his mishap; and in his heart, no doubt cursing and doubly cursing the quarterdeck fool, and gradually pulls round to shore again, and the girls are not sparing of their epithets on the occasion. Here the waterman is a loser, for he takes them conditionally: that is, if they are made choice, of, or what he calls sold, he receives three shillings each; and, if not, then no pay,—he has his labour for his pains; at least these were the terms at Portsmouth and Plymouth in war-time, at these great naval depots. A boat usually carries about ten of these poor creatures at a time, and will often bring off three cargoes of these ladies in a day; so that, if he is fortunate in his sales, as he calls them, he will make nearly five pounds by his three trips. Thus these poor unfortunates are taken to market like cattle; and, whilst this system is observed, it cannot with truth be said, that the slave-trade is abolished in England.

I am now happily laid up in matrimonial harbour, blest in a wife and several children, and my constant prayer to heaven is, that my daughters may never step a foot on board of a man-of-war.

It may seem strange to many persons, that seamen before the mast should be allowed to have those ladies on board; whilst the officers must not, on pain of being tried by a court-martial, for disobedience of orders, the Admiralty having made a regulation to that effect. The reason of this is, that the seamen are not allowed to go on shore, but the officers are, and may partake of what pleasure they choose.

Whilst on this subject, I will just mention an occurrence which took place on board a ship then lying at Spithead: one of the seamen said to his messmate, that he should like to have a cruise on shore before he went to sea again, and would contrive it by asking permission of the captain to go and get married. This was a poser, for the captain, as he dare not well refuse it, if there would be time for it. The captain having doubts as to the truth of the application, sent a Sergeant and a file of marines on shore with him, to see that he did get married, and with orders to bring him on board so soon as the ceremony was over. Here poor Jack was quite taken a-back, for this was a step he did not expect would have been taken by the captain; but as it was so, why he'd make the best of it. Whilst he was being pulled to shore, he was pondering what he had best do;—his spirit did not like to be detected in a falsehood; but this was the truck of all tricks he had ever met with. He had no time to waver, and the thought struck him. He had money enough in his pocket to pay for a licence, but what to do for a wife he know not. Bent on keeping up his credit for veracity with the captain, he resolved upon asking the first girl he should meet, and if she refused, to ask another, until he had found one. Upon getting on shore, it so happened that the first one accepted his invitation; he instantly bought a ring procured a license, and they were married at Kingston church, near Portsmouth. It cannot be said on this, as it is on most similar occasions, that, "the happy pair passed the honey-moon together;" for he was immediately hurried on board again; and the ship weighed anchor for sea, without his having another interview with his newly-made bride, or even knowing where she lived: such shocks as these are British seamen liable to meet, where a captain has no feeling for a fellow-creature. Enrobed with the character of wife, she would not keep him long in ignorance as to her residence, for the sake of the half-pay; and she would make it convenient, no doubt, to obtain a Certificate of the marriage without delay; for this would be very useful, as it would protect her at all times against the occasional order of the mayor, to turn all the loose single women out of the town.

Pay-day on Board

Our ship having been in dock, she was prepared and got ready for sea again. A day or two previous to our sailing, the ship's crew was paid agreeably to an Admiralty order, and, to picture the scenes, which at this time occurred, is a task almost impossible. In the early part of the day the commissioners came on board, bringing the money which is paid the ship's crew, with the exception of six months pay, which it is the rule of the government to hold back from each man. The mode of paying is, as the names are, by rotation on the books: every man, when called, is asked for his hat, which is returned to him with his wages in it, and the amount chalked on the rim. There is not perhaps one in twenty who actually knows what he is going to receive,. nor does the particular amount seem to be a matter of much concern; for, when paid, they hurry down to their respective berths, redeem their honour with their several ladies and bomb-boat men, and then they turn their thoughts to the Jew peddlers, who are ranged round the decks and on the hatch-way gratings, in fact, the ship is crowded with them. They are furnished with every article that will rig out a sailor, never omitting, in their parkains, a fine large watch and appendages, all warranted, and with which many an honest tar has been taken in: they can supply them likewise with fashionable rings and trinkets for their ladies, of pure gold, oh! nothing can be purer! Yet with all Mordecai's asseverations, its purity may be doubted.

One of our men, after having been paid, in taking a ramble round the deck, thinking how he should lay out more of his money; went down to his berth, and told his mess-mate, that there was one of the Jews on board, of whom he had formerly bought a silver watch, and so had several of his ship-mates, for five guineas each, but none of them would go long unless carried; his messmate advised him to go and bargain for a jacket, waistcoat, and trousers, and when he had got them on, and looking to see how they should fit, the other was to act the part of boatswain's mate, by coming behind him with a rope's end, and begin to start him with it, at the same time calling him a skulking rascal: the plan succeeded, the man, on being cut at with the rope's-end, snatched up his old garments, and ran down the after-hatchway, with the pretended boatswain's mate after him; the Jew confidently expecting the man would return and pay him for the suit of clothes; for, being at the time busily employed in selling his goods, he did not make enquiry until the evening, when the Jews were all ordered out of the ship; he then made it known to the captain, who caused enquiry to be made: the boatswain's mates were called aft, but none of them knew of a man having been started at the time the Jew mentioned; the captain then told Moses that he could do no more for him, unless the men who had played off the trick were brought to him, and then he would take care they should be punished.

On this promise the Jew went below; he looked with piercing eyes between the guns fore and aft, where the men mess, but could not find the sculker who had so ingeniously taken his revenge, and possessed himself of a suit of clothes. Mortified to think he should be so done, he swore, by Moses and the Prophets, he would find the villain; became exasperated, and left the ship, amidst the grins and jeers of the whole crew, who were much diverted and pleased to think that any of their shipmates had tact enough to retaliate so nicely on a Jew.

The word was now passed for the women to stand by, and be ready to go on shore the next day. It is not the happiest moment of a sailor's life, when he has to part with his Nancy, but grieving's a folly, and, upon these occasions they generally throw grief and a temporary affection over the taffrail, as commodities they do not take to sea with them. The boats being ready alongside, some of our men, being full of frolic and fun, had bought bunches of onions and turnips, and would very politely offer a few of the onions to those ladies who could not contrive to get up a cry at parting, without their aid; and, in their cruelty, would add a turnip or two, signifying that they were turned adrift: this creates a little merriment with a great portion of the ship's company, and is generally taken in good part by the ladies, who are accustomed to such gambols, and whose hearts are not very sensible of the tender passions; however, the next day at parting, there were a few who felt the separation with concern; here and there one man would appear chap-fallen; another would heave a sigh; and some were waving their hands; whilst others might be seen to drop a tear, as a dozen or two had plunged themselves into matrimony during the time we were in harbour, and of course felt as proper on the occasion, when parting from their wives, and not being able to calculate when they might meet again.

To Sea again

Our captain having left us, we were joined by another, and the ship put to sea, and we soon found that we had become Channel gropers, a term given to the Channel fleet in war time, which is destined to hover about Brest when the wind is fair for the French fleet to come out, as we were blockading them; and when the wind blows strong into the harbour, so that they could not well get out; in those cases, our fleet would sometimes put in at Cawsand or Torbay, and might be what sailors call a fresh beef station, but it is such as few seamen like, for they say it is neither being abroad nor at home. One reason why they have a dislike to it is, that they are open to the ridicule of seamen who may be coming from foreign stations, as well as by the girls and people in the sea-port towns by cantingly telling them they would never have the scurvy, or that they might as well be by their mother's fire-side, and tied to the apron-strings, as merely running in and out of harbour; and nothing hurts Jack's feelings more than being taunted of anything unmanly or inferior. Some captains have, however, a fondness for the apron-string station, and this might, with much justice, have been said of our old woman of a captain; he was an M. P., of high birth, had great influence at head quarters, and was fond of being placed near home: he was constantly taking his trips to London, whenever he pleased, leaving the command of the ship in the hands of the first lieutenant, who was a tyrant on board, and was sure to be supported by this (M. P.) captain, who flogged every man that was reported to him by the aforesaid lieutenant, without enquiring into the complaint, for that would have been beneath his dignity as a man and an officer. This sort of conduct had nearly brought the ship into a state of mutiny, and indeed many of our men ran away. He was so much the lofty high-spirited gentleman, that he would not condescend to command the ship when he was on board, but would leave it in the hands of the lieutenant, so that, as to the discharge of duty as an officer, he might as well have been on shore. He was so independent, and so much the man of pleasure, that he had never been through the ship to examine the state of it, or the crew: he had his band on board, to the amount of upwards of twenty performers, sending as many prime seamen away, and having this musical junto in their stead, and thus weakening our force; for these worthies were excused from the ship's duty; they were rated as petty officers, or able seamen, and received pay as such, whilst the men who were actually doing the ship's duty were some rated as landsmen, and others as ordinary seamen. As a band, these gentlemen were kept fully employed, for whilst he was indulging himself in the cabin with the importance of a great bashaw, they would be playing at the door; for this band and his dog drew all his attention, and seemed to be his sole delight: he was pompous, proud, imperious, unfeeling, and, of course, detested.

Whilst lying in Torbay, with the fleet, an order came for our ship to weigh anchor for Plymouth, and there take in supplies for the L'Orient squadron; and having done so, we sailed, but with a substitute or supernumerary captain instead of our nautical grand vizier, he being in London, attending on his parliamentary duties. On rounding the French land, by Brest, we discovered the fleet out, and standing towards L'Orient; our ship being the only English one in sight, and they being eight sail of the line, together with some small craft, we kept about two leagues distance during the greater part of the day; having on board a number of live bullocks, as well as other provision, our butcher was ordered to kill them ready for throwing overboard in case of coming to action.

As night was drawing on, we discovered our blockading squadron off L'Orient, consisting of three sail of the line, and as we neared them, we fired a gun, and let fly the topgallant-sheet, which is a signal for an enemy; and in a short time joined them. At this time we were about a gun-shot to leeward of the enemy, and expected they would have engaged us; but it was nearly dark, and we afterwards learned that their lower-deck ports were barred, in consequence of their being closely stowed with provisions, destined for the relief of one of their West India Islands.

The night had set in very dark, we kept making signals to a look-out brig during the night; but when the morning appeared they were like the "Flying

Dutchman," invisible to us—they had escaped our vigilance. Consternation seized the commodore: it was all helter-skelter—pell-mell—all in the wrong—the devil to pay, and no pitch hot: indeed his tongue was lying to under a storm jib. He began to telegraph, "Which way have they steered?" and we were chasing and bringing to, every thing like a ship we could see upon the water: and at length we got a clue that they were seen near Rochfort. We made sail, bent our course for that place, and soon joined our blockading squadron, when we learned that the enemy had run in, making together thirteen sail of the line, besides frigates and gun-brigs.

While we were blockading them with seven sail of the line, and two or three small craft, a frigate happened to join us, and an expedient was immediately resorted to, to deceive the enemy; for she was rose upon with canvas in the course of the night, and painted chequered-sided, to make her have the appearance of a line-of-battle ship at a distance, and by this manoeuvre, the French thought that we were eight sail of the line; and thus we kept them in, until we were joined by some other ships, amongst which was the Caledonian, with Lord Gambier as Commander-in-Chief. We now anchored in their outer-roads, or as the French call it, the Basque Roads; and Lord Gambier thought that it would be very advisable that some fire-ships should be employed to destroy the enemy at their anchorage, instead of our going in, to engage them; but Admiral Harvey was of opinion, that it might have been effected by the fleet we then had with us; and such was the idea entertained by nineteen out of every twenty composing the fleet. Admiral Harvey suggested to Lord Gambier, the propriety of engaging the enemy directly, rather than give them time to escape to their inner harbour, where we could not by any means get at them, on account of the batteries. Admiral Harvey's plan was to form our fleet in two divisions: the one to attack and take the Isle D'Aix, which commands the harbour by its strong batteries; and the other was to engage the French shipping and amuse it until the island surrendered, and then this division to join and give its assistance; and with aid from the batteries, their whole fleet would inevitably have fallen into our possession; but the suggestion, however solid, however feasible, yet it was not approved of by the Commander-in-Chief: notwithstanding, so sanguine was Admiral Harvey of its success, and being second in command, offered to lead either division to the enterprise. The plea of the Commander-in-Chief was, that it would be a great risk of men's lives; and yet, he could prepare to adopt the mode of destroying them by fire ships; and if that idea had been carried into effect to the full extent of its object, we should not only have burnt their shipping, but also the crews in them must have become sacrificed; and though it were an enemy, yet the thought is shuddering, that nearly ten thousand men, whilst they were harmlessly asleep in their cots and hammocks, might be roasted to death, and perhaps without a moment's time to say, "Lord have mercy upon me!" and how the Commander-in-Chief, could express himself as to the fear of taking away life, with this murderous plot on his brain, is inconceivable, and a strange reason for not agreeing to the proposition which had been made to him.

Admiral Harvey having been one of the Nelson school, and seeing the enemy within our reach, happened to express himself rather too warmly, at not being allowed to engage them. This gave great umbrage to the Commander-in-Chief, and for which he was sent home, tried, and broke; but re-instated at the bottom of the list of Admirals. This must have been no very comfortable reflection for one who had often signalized himself, and on one occasion so gallantly repulsed the enemy, when boarded on each side by him, and whose ship suffered more than any other of the fleet at the battle of Trafalgar; and who felt as an Englishman and an officer, and was well satisfied that he possessed the means to capture the French fleet, without recourse to the hazardous, expensive, and doubtful expedient of fire-ships: however, orders were given, and fire-ships was to be the mode of warfare. Having several merchant vessels with us, from two to three hundred tons burthen, each man-of-war was to fit out one of these as a fire-ship; and we had also one much larger, which was the Mediator store-ship, which was successful in breaking the bar placed across the entrance, to prevent our ships getting in. After they were all prepared and made ready, the wind being fair, the signal was made to weigh anchor, and proceed to the work of destruction. Notwithstanding all this preparation, as the cruel substitute for a manly engagement, it did not exactly answer the helm of the admiral's expectations, for not one of the fire-ships ran near enough to catch hold of the enemy's rigging with the grapplings; it certainly frightened, for they cut their cables, and ran up to the inner harbour, with the exception of four line-of-battle ships, that got aground; but to affright them was not the object, it was not conquest.

Here was exhibited a grand display of fire-works, at the expense of John Bull; no gala night at Ranelagh or Vauxhall, could be compared to it. Our fleet was lying quite composedly at a distance, with the crews in and about the rigging, for the greater part of the night, witnessing the effects of the Congreve rockets, as well as the explosion of each fire-ship, which illuminated the air, one after the other.

However dangerous the service, yet there are never wanting British seamen to embark in it, and on this occasion a boat's-crew, from each ship of the line, volunteered their services to take those fire-ships in: it is a sort of forlorn hope adventure, for every man taken on such an expedition, by the enemy, is liable to be dealt with in a similar manner as a spy, and put to death: it is a mode of warfare dreadful to resort to, and should not be practised by any civilised nation. Those who are so fortunate as to return safe, were generally, at least in most cases, promoted.

On daylight appearing, in the morning of the 12th of April, we discovered the four French ships aground; and two frigates and a bomb vessel were sent in, under the command of Lord Cochrane, to destroy them, or to ascertain the means by which it could be effected. This was a task which just suited his lordship's taste, and that he was well calculated to carry into execution: for he commenced raking and firing away directly he got in; but the contest was a very unequal one; his lordship should have had a greater force with him. The captains and officers of the different ships were much hurt on the occasion, and might be seen to walk the decks, biting their lips, with regret at not being allowed to go and assist the frigates: at length our ship asked permission to afford them our aid; and the admiral gave his consent that ourselves and another line-of-battle ship to go to his lordship's assistance; our anchor in a second kissed the bows, was stowed, and the ship in full sail in the twinkling of an eye; in fact, never was seen such dispatch, so great was the anxiety of all hands to be busy. In a very short time we anchored in their harbour, between the batteries and the shipping, and commenced pouring our broadsides so rapidly into the French ships aground, that they became an easy conquest: two of them struck to us, and the other two to the frigates.

Our ship having touched the ground, we were obliged to lay under their batteries all night, and had they been skilful marksmen, they must have cut us to pieces; their shots were whistling over us, some a-stern, and a great many fell short: there was not one in fifty that hit us, but those that did, effected great execution. Amongst them was a very distressing and mischievous one, which knocked a man's head completely from his shoulders, and struck a lieutenant on the breast: the lieutenant was knocked down by the force of the head striking him; he was of course taken down to the cock-pit as a wounded man from his being very much be-smeared with the blood from the man's head. The doctor immediately enquired of him, where about he was hurt, and he pointed to his breast; but when the doctor unbuttoned his waistcoat and examined, there was not the least symptom of his having been wounded; indeed he was more frightened than hurt, but certainly it was enough to alarm any man. He was requested to sit down and compose himself, and to state the truth, it was some time before that fit of composure went off, for he very prudently had no notion of going on deck again, while men's heads were flying about, and doing so much mischief. Nearly twenty of our men were killed and wounded, and among them was a steady and much respected seaman, with the calves of both his legs shot away. It became necessary to amputate one of the legs immediately, and during the operation he did not utter a syllable; and shortly after, on the doctor's examining the other leg, that was also doomed to undergo a similar fate; upon being told this, the poor fellow pleaded very hard that it might be left him, and very coolly observed that he should like one leg left to wear his shoes out, but the doctor was obliged to take off the other leg, the symptoms of mortification being very apparent: like a brave fellow, he bore his sufferings with great fortitude, and to the surprise of every one present at the finish of the second amputation, he exclaimed, "now to the devil with all the shoe-makers, I have done with them!" This man was progressively doing well, and his wounds were healing fast; but, from lying in one position for such a length of time, his back mortified, and he breathed his last, much regretted by all his shipmates.

I will now return to the four French ships we had possessed ourselves of; the prisoners were taken out, and we set fire to them, on the night of the 13th of April, and they gradually burnt until the fire reached the magazines, when they blew up with a tremendous shock, but it was awfully grand: after the destruction of these four ships, we were ordered home to repair our damage and re-fit.

In Old England once again

On arriving in England, our great swell, and M. P. captain took the command again, and the man who had so gallantly fought our ship, was turned adrift; he was a noble fellow, although of no high family or titled connections; but valour, without these appendages, is not always sure of meeting its reward, at least in this instance it did not, for Admiralty promotion is a difficult canvas.

After refitting our ship at Portsmouth, we were ordered to prepare for the reception of troops on board for a secret expedition. Every vessel, both ships of war and transports, that could be got hold of, was detained and employed to form this grand armament. Spithead appeared like a floating: forest of masts; the Downs were in a like manner, crowded with a part of this armada; indeed every thing was life and bustle, our harbours and roadsteads were one scene of industrious preparation. At the gangway nothing was heard but major such-a-one's, and colonel such-a-one's luggage alongside, for our captain being an M. P. of the pompous cast, he of course, was much gratified by having persons of rank and title as cabin companions; and it seemed, as though that fine feathers and glittering swords were to secure success to this grand enterprise.

The Walcherin Expedition

At length we sailed, and Walcherin was our destination; had we been a fleet of Liliputians going to attack a Gulliver, we were numerous enough to have killed and eaten him, and to have towed the island home afterwards. Our force was near forty sail of the line, besides frigates, sloops, and gun-brigs, making altogether upwards of one hundred and thirty ships of war, besides gun-boats and transports, full a thousand in number; and the military force consisted of forty thousand men.

Having arrived at Walcherin, we commenced disembarking the troops, at about five o'clock in the morning, previously serving every man with three days provisions, or rations as the soldiers call them. On reaching the land, some of the horses' and men's feet were unexpectedly cut with iron spikes, which had been ingeniously placed in the grass and cow fields for that purpose by the enemy.

Having completed our disembarkation, the ships of war anchored at a distance from the island, and remained inactive for nearly a fortnight: the small-arms men, from different ships of the line, were sent ashore to assist the troops, and also to be employed in throwing up fortifications and erecting batteries: whilst this was going on, the military and some of the naval officers, were regaling themselves at Middleburgh, which is an inland town, and is the capital; Sir William Curtis having just then arrived in his yacht, and had brought plenty of turtle with him, it is easy to imagine that there was no lack of feasting, lounging, and parading about: some of the military were at this hour employed in driving the enemy's sharpshooters from the thickets and bushes; and here they had a fine opportunity of gathering plenty of apples, as they were growing spontaneously and in abundance, on different parts of the island.

Many of our people, by eating too freely of the this fruit, were apt to drink to an excess of the hollands, and would incautiously lay down to sleep on the earth, when, from the dampness of the atmosphere, the island laying low, and interspersed with a number of canals, it caused an ague to follow, and a number of lives were lost, who unhappily fell victims to their imprudence.

Our newly erected batteries being now completed, a summons was sent in for the town of Flushing to surrender; to this the commandant sent in a negative, unless compelled by the force of arms: a second message was then sent, requesting that the women and children might be sent away, as the intention was to bombard the town, and it would be desirable that their lives should not become the sacrifice; and the commandant's reply was, that he would not allow any person to leave the town.

The time given having expired, we commenced an attack upon the town, and during the bombardment, one of our batteries had unfortunately an explosion of powder, which killed and wounded several of our men. I will here remark, that on one of the sallies made by the enemy out of the gates of the town, the soldiers and small-arm-men from the ships, were employed in engaging them, and the small-arms-men being seamen, with an impetuosity not to be controlled, they rushed on the enemy with such rapidity, while the military were waiting the word of command, that they actually drove the enemy within the gates of the town, with the loss of a very few lives, at the same time vociferating that the soldiers should not go before them to battle. Several times during the conflict, the soldiers would have fired on the enemy, but could not, for fear of killing our seamen.

After destroying a great portion of the town, by shots, shells, and rockets, it surrendered; and on our taking possession, the sight was melancholy and distressing to behold. There was scarcely a street but in which the greater part of the houses were knocked down, with women and children buried under their ruins. Some were dug out scarcely alive and much mutilated, whilst others found a ready grave amidst the devastation. One third of the town was completely destroyed, and other parts much damaged; even the church did not escape, it received much injury by catching fire.

Being in the habit of going ashore two or three times a week, I had an opportunity of ascertaining somewhat the feelings of the inhabitants: and I found, naturally enough too, that they were much prejudiced against the English, who certainly did their duty with fidelity to their king and country. On one occasion, I called at an ironmonger's to buy a lock, and on endeavouring to make myself understood, a female in the shop spoke to me in English, and in our conversation, she stated that she was a native of Poole, in Dorsetshire; that she had been married and had resided there some years: she had lost her husband at one of the attacks on the town, which had frequently been besieged, owing to the contentions of the different European nations, so that it frequently changed owners, and had, but a short time before, been in possession of the French. Notwithstanding her being an English woman, she could not help saying, but that she wished us away; for the price of provisions was generally enhanced, in consequence of our visit, to such an extent, that they could scarcely afford to keep body and soul together, from the exorbitant prices.

The roaring of cannon having subsided, and the din of war, with all its horrors, being heard no more, the Commander-in-Chief, and his colleagues, together with the naval officers, enjoyed a little leisure, and made a grand display in the town; nothing was to be seen but red coats and blue coats, epaulettes and feathers; there were, however, a few of the naval officers, who could not join in these lounges, as they were employed to superintend the taking to pieces of one ship, and launching another to be sent to England. It fell to our lot to be ordered home, with near seven hundred prisoners; there were some of all nations - French, Dutch, Russians, Prussians, Austrians, Danes, Swedes, and a sprinkle of Spaniards.

There was with one of the Spaniards the curious circumstance of a musket ball, that had struck him, and was lodged between the lower lip and chin; it must have been what is termed, "a spent ball," or it would have shattered his face to pieces. It had not injured the jaw-bone, and the skin had healed over it. He had received it, he said, whilst fighting in Spain, and did not seem to feel any inconvenience from it. He observed that many medical men, had been very anxious, and had offered their kind services, to relieve him, of what he called his chapfallen companion, and to make a sound cure; for though not attended with pain, it was working down to the under part of the chin; but he said it was an honorable badge, and, as a trophy, he would carry it to his grave.

Having landed our prisoners in England, we were ordered again to Flushing, and there remained until the English evacuated the place, which was near the Christmas of 1809. Previous to our coming away, we did all the mischief we could; we set fire to every thing in the dock-yard, and filled up the entrance of the different canals with stones and rubbish; this obtained for us no good name, for on leaving, we were much ridiculed and jeered by the Dutchmen, who exclaimed that we had brought a large force there, and had done nothing worthy of war, but to knock down their houses, and distress the poor inhabitants, and this was partly true: it was certainly a great error that the naval force was not allowed to make the attack until the army could act with it; for we could have taken very nearly all the Dutch shipping then lying abreast of Flushing, together with the town, without aid either from the army, transports, or flat-bottomed-boats, the ships of war, and men being so numerous; instead of which, the enemy were allowed to run up the river to Antwerp, coolly, and at their pleasure; whilst we were obliged to come away without having obtained our object. To be sure some hundreds of men's lives were sacrificed; and, as we were told on our arrival in England, that nearly twenty millions of money had been expended on that expedition.

If any thing can lower the spirits of the British sailor, it is that of not being able to speak triumphantly of any enterprise he may have been upon; and certainly, on our return from this formidably prepared undertaking, we had nothing to reflect on that could gladden the heart, or be the cause of exultation; but, on the contrary, disappointment was seen to hang upon every man's and he was ashamed to own, whither he had been. When accosted, and talked to, they would generally try to waive or elude the subject; they were sneered at, and saluted with the sarcastic title, of *"The grand secret expedition men:— yes? they'll let us into the secret too by and by, in the way of a side wind heavy taxation;"* and this sort of ungenerous taunting, did not help to dispel the cloud, in which their minds would be enveloped; they were compelled to bear it, but with regret.

Channel Gropers again

On board the different ships, there were numerous packages, which had been shipped at Flushing, and no doubt, but they were intended to be smuggled into England, from the secret manner, and the different stratagems used, in the getting of them afterwards on shore: the bread-room of our ship was crowded with them, directed for different officers holding high rank, both in army and navy: and may have been intended as presents, or for their own use; But they did not pay the duty. These packages consisted of, sets of Hamburg china, and table services, down for beds, spirits, and various other articles, of foreign produce. Not being able to land all these goods at once, without detection, we contrived it at different intervals, safely thus got rid of some of them by different conveyances, and then we became Channel Gropers again; and whilst on this duty, we landed the balance of our secret cargo, at Weymouth and Plymouth, as we were frequently running into those ports.

Whilst on the Cherbourgh blockade station, it often

occurred that we were in chase of vessels, supposing them to be smugglers, and at the same time, we were meditating how to get rid of the bulk of our bread-room stowage, which did not intend to pay any duty, for we had his Majesty's pendant which no custom-house officer searches so strictly. Contrast this with a seaman's bringing home the most trifling article, as a present to a relation or friend: the poor fellow is pounced upon immediately, and compelled to submit to the laws of his country, whilst the other, holding his Majesty's commission, by the aid of his lieutenant, and his boat's crews, commits a flagrant act of smuggling with impunity; but the poor seaman, if taken, is sure to suffer.

It would savour more of propriety if the revenue officers were a little more vigilant, and kept an eye upon those who are paid to prevent infractions, instead of being the first violators of our laws.

Whilst we were keeping a good look out for some French privateers, that would now and then creep out in hazy weather or dark nights, we happened to fall in with and took one of them. She had a fine crew on board, who had enriched themselves by intercepting and capturing our homeward bound West Indiamen, when running up channel, for sugar was at that time nearly 5s. per lb. From them we learned that Bonaparte had ordered the growth of beet root to be proceeded with, from which a sugar was extracted, as France had lost her West India colonies, and the whole of her ports were blockaded, as their principal supply was from their privateers, or occasionally by an American evading our blockading squadron, and getting into one of their ports with a cargo.

Having learned that a French frigate had escaped from their harbour, and had taken shelter under the batteries of La Hogue, we went in with a determination to engage and bring her out, if possible. On opening our fire upon her, the batteries commenced a well-directed fire upon us, and so violent, that we were obliged to abandon her; and on tacking ship to come out, we were shot like the Leviathan* on the first of June; for an awkward shot came in at one of the after port-holes, and took away five legs from bodies of three of the men who were working the gun. Two of the unfortunate brave fellows died; the other survived after suffering the amputation of both legs above where they were shattered. This man we had pressed out of a homeward-bound East-Indiaman a few days before. On his application to the Admiralty afterwards with his papers, he was told he had not been long enough in the service; they did not see what they could do for him; but, by persevering, on a second application, twenty pounds per annum were granted to him.

* *The Leviathan, of 74 guns, was part of the fleet that Lord Howe had under him when he obtained a glorious victory over the French, on the 1st of June, 1794, and was so completely raked that her stern was entirely shot in; and it has been ever since a common saying, when a ship has been violently raked she was shot just like the Leviathan.*

Ordered to Lisbon

Soon after this, we were ordered to prepare the ship to take troops for Lisbon, destined to join Lord Wellington, he being much, at that time, in want of reinforcements. On this order arriving, our M. P. captain again left us. After getting five thousand troops on board of the different ships, we sailed, but were obliged to put into Torbay, the wind blowing up channel so strong that we were detained several days. This was a fine opportunity for our seamen to feast themselves on bullock's liver, or Torbay goose, as they call it; for this, fried with salt pork, makes not only a relishing, but a delicious meal for a mess: indeed, it has frequently occurred, that our captain would, when we were killing a bullock at sea, send orders to the butcher for his cook to be supplied with a plate of the liver, to be fried for his table. At Torquay, a town in Torbay, it has been usual in wartime to kill for a supply of beef to the channel fleet, and then we often partook of this very excellent dish, as the livers were plentiful.

The wind having at last veered round, we weighed anchor, and ran down channel; but we were buffeted about in the Bay of Biscay for three weeks by contrary winds and a heavy swell of sea. This was a distressing time for the poor soldiers and their wives, who were unaccustomed to such tossing and tumbling about, many of whom would be rolling into the lee-scuppers, when the ship would take a lurch that way; and if it should be so unfortunate as to happen when they were fetching their grog or pea soup, all would go to leeward; for a heavy sea shows no favour; and this would be a loss severely felt by them, for they were, to use the sea phrase, living six upon four; that is, they were only served out with two-thirds of a seaman's allowance: and such an accident cannot be remedied, as vain would be an application to the purser for a re-supply.

After a tedious voyage, we at length arrived at Lisbon, which was in the year 1811, and no time was lost in disembarking the troops. During our stay at this place, we witnessed the extreme sentence of the law being put into execution upon two marines, who were hung at the yardarm of one of His Majesty's ships, for no other offence but that of throwing an officer overboard who had used them cruelly at different times. It will be said, that they deserved the fate they met, as they had no right to take the law into their own hands; but, in mitigation of such a reproach to their memory, let the reader recollect, that these poor fellows had no other means of redress: and it is a proof how much a reform is wanted in the conduct of officers both in the navy and the marines.

Having safely landed our freight, and bearing no orders to go on any particular service, we prepared for our return to old England, and arrived at Portsmouth in the latter end of the year, when I quitted, and took my leave of the naval service.

Postscript

The career of a youthful nautical frolic being ended, the mind has had time to reflect, and by an examination of the past, it has prepared me somewhat to shape my course for the future, as experience is the best teacher. In contemplating the varied scenes of so motley a profession as that of a sailor, there is much to be thought on with pleasure, and much with a bitter anguish and disgust. To the youth possessing any thing of a roving disposition it is attractive, nay, it is seducing; for it has its allurements, and when steadily pursued and with success, it ennobles the mind, and the seaman feels himself a man. There is, indeed, no profession that can vie with it; and a British seaman has a right to be proud, for he is incomparable when placed alongside those of any other nation. Great Britain can truly boast of her hearts of oak, the floating sinews of her existence, and the high station she holds in the political world; and if she could but once rub out those stains of wanton and torturing punishments, so often unnecessarily resorted to, and abandon the unnatural and uncivilized custom of impressment, then, and not till then, can her navy be said to have got to the truck of perfection. In the first, a radical reform in her officers is the only means to effect it; for did these men but think a little more of national honor, and a little less of self-importance, there would be less difference between the belly and the members. A seaman will as soon risk his life for his kind and good captain, as he would to defend his country's honor; but among the many who have had command in the British navy, how few there are who are spoken well of by those who have sailed with them. One instance alone will show the disparity.

How happy must that officer be, who has the consolation to know that he was beloved by his ship's company, and as proof of it, may, at the end of a voyage, have presented to him by the crew, as a token of their regard and esteem, a gold cup or a piece of plate, with the honest sentiments of those brave fellows' respect and attachment engraved on it. Out of a fleet of nine sail of the line I was with, there were only two captains thus distinguished. They kept order on board without resorting to the frequent and unnecessary call upon the boatswain and his cat, adopted by the other seven; and what was the consequence? Those two ships beat us in reefing and furling; for they were not in fear and dread, well knowing they would not be punished without a real and just cause. Those men would have stormed a battery, or have engaged an enemy at sea, with more vigour and effect than the other seven; for the crews of those seven felt themselves so degraded at being wantonly and unmanly beaten about, that their spirits were partly broken; and in going to battle, the only thing that could stimulate, cheer, and inspire them, was not veneration for their commanders, but the recollection of the land that gave them birth, Old England.

I am convinced that no civilized society can be maintained, and order preserved in it, unless a due observance of its laws are preserved, and subordination is kept up; but in these enlightened times, cruelty surely need not be the means resorted to for the enforcement of obedience. In giving this narrative, I am not actuated by malice, my motive and object arises from a wish to see some enactment, that those men who are England's safeguard, the defenders of her honour and glory, should be used as men—not as brutes; and that some plan should be devised to procure seamen, without impressment;— then, and not till then, will an Englishman be able to say, that he was born in the land of freedom. On these two points the following pages will be employed, merely stating facts, leaving an enlightened public to form its opinion, and trusting to the Legislature for some wise and salutary enactment on these important points, so essential to the happiness and welfare of the nation.

The Different Modes of Punishment in the British Navy

Any person who has been on board a ship of war, must be aware that discipline and subordination is necessary, but the extent to which cruelty was carried on under the name of discipline, on board many ships during the late war, is not generally known, nor will a British public believe that any body of men would submit to such marks of degradation as they were compelled to undergo.

It was partially known at Somerset House by the different ships' logs, but the real crime, if any, was not, it is believed, therein set down; for there it all came under the head of "disobedience;" or under a peculiar article of war, which runs as follows:—"All crimes not capital shall be punished according to the customs and manners used at sea."

This article shelters the captains in the navy in resorting to almost any mode of punishment they may think proper.

Flogging through the Fleet

Whilst lying at Spithead, in the year 1809 or 1810, four impressed seamen attempted to make their escape from a frigate, then lying there; one of their shipmates, a Dutchman, to whom they had entrusted the secret, betrayed their intention, and informed the commanding officer of their designs. They were tried by a court-martial, and sentenced to receive three hundred lashes, each through the fleet. On the first day after the trial that the weather was moderate enough to permit, the signal was made for a boat from each ship, with a guard of marines, to attend the punishment. The man is placed in a launch, *i.e.* the largest ships' boat, under the care of the master-at-arms and a doctor. There is a capstern bar rigged fore and aft, to which this poor fellow is lashed by his wrists, and for fear of hurting him—humane creatures—there is a stocking put over each, to prevent him from tearing the flesh off in his agonies. When all is ready, the prisoner is stript and seized to the capstern bar. Punishment commences by the officer, after reading the sentence of the court-martial, ordering the boatswains' mates to do their duty. The cat-of-nine-tails is applied to the bare back, and at about every six lashes, a fresh boatswain's mate is ordered to relieve the executioner of this duty, until the prisoner has received, perhaps, twenty-five lashes: he is then cast loose, and allowed to sit down with a blanket rolled round him, is conveyed to the next ship, escorted by this vast number of armed boats, accompanied by that doleful music, "the rogues' march." In this manner he is conveyed from ship to ship, receiving alongside of each a similar number of stripes with the cat, until the sentence is completed. It often, nay generally, happens, that nature is unable to sustain it, and the poor fellow faints and sinks under it, although every kind method is made use of to enable him to bear it, by pouring wine down his throat. The doctor will then feel his pulse, and often pronounces that the man is unable to bear more. He is then taken, most usually insensible, to what is termed the sick bay; and, if he recovers, he is told he will have to receive the remainder of his punishment. When there are many ships in the fleet at the time of the court-martial, this ceremony, if the prisoner can sustain it, will last nearly half the day.

On the blanket being taken from his back, and he supported or lifted to be lashed to the capstern-bar, after he has been alongside of several ships, his back resembles so much putrefied liver, and every stroke of the cat brings away the congealed blood; and the boatswains' mates are looked at with the eye of a hawk to see they do their duty, and clear the cat's tails after every stroke, the blood at the time streaming through their fingers: and in this manner are men in the navy punished for different offences, more particularly impressed men, who attempt to make their escape. The court that awards this punishment is composed of naval captains or commanders, the judge is a naval officer, and the accuser is a naval officer. One of those men after the trial, when addressed by one of his messmates with "I was sorry to hear you were found guilty; I was in hopes you would have been acquitted."

"So I should have been," was his reply, "had I been tried by a jury of seamen: indeed, I am sure I cannot go through the torture; I would rather have been sentenced to be shot, or hung at the yard-arm; aye, and for my only attempting to escape after having been impressed."

Running the Gauntlet

This is a punishment inflicted for any petty theft. The criminal is placed with his naked back in a large tub, wherein a seat has been fixed, and his hands lashed down to the sides: this tub is secured on a grating, and is drawn round the decks by the boys, the master-at-arms with his drawn sword pointing to the prisoner's breast. The cavalcade starts from the break of the quarter-deck, after the boatswain has given the prisoner a dozen lashes, and the ship's crew are ranged round the decks in two rows, so that the prisoner passes between them, and each man is provided with a three yarn nettle; that is, three rope yarns tightly laid together and knotted. With this, each man must cut him, or be thought implicated in the theft. Six boatswains' mates give him half a dozen each, as he passes round the decks, so that he receives four dozen lashes from the boatswain and his mates with a cat-o'-nine tails, and six hundred cuts with the three yarn nettle from the crew of a line of battle ship, that being the average number of men before the mast in war time. This punishment is inflicted by the captain's orders, without the formal inquiry by a court-martial.

Flogging at the Gangway or on the Quarter-Deck

The captain orders this punishment for any thing that himself or any of his officers may consider as a crime. The prisoner is made to strip to his waist; he is then seized by his wrists and knees to a grating or ladder; the boatswain's mate is then ordered to cut him with the cat-o'-nine tails; and after six or twelve lashes are given, another boatswain's mate is called to continue the exercise; and so they go on, until the captain gives the word to stop. From one to five dozen lashes are given, according to the captain's whim, but the general number is three dozen; and this number the captain has power to give every day, if he has any bad feeling for an individual: and a tyrant of a captain will frequently tell the boatswain's mate to lay it on harder, or that he should be flogged next himself. This punishment is also inflicted without trial by court-martial, at the discretion of the captain. It is not so in the army.

Starting

This may be carried to a great extent of torture, as every boatswain's mate carries a rope's-end in his pocket; it is part of their equipment; and when ordered to start the men by any of the officers, they must not be found wanting of that appendage. The man is ordered to pull off" his jacket, and sometimes his waistcoat, if he has one on at the time; the boatswain's mate then commences beating him, and continues to do so until he is ordered to stop, or unless his arm is tired, and then another boatswain's mate is called to go on with the ceremony. Some of those men's backs have often been so bad from the effects of the starting system, that they have not been able to bear their jackets on for several days: and as this punishment is inflicted without tying the men up, he will naturally endeavour to ward off or escape as many of the blows as possible, and in doing so he frequently gets a serious cut in the face or head. This punishment is so common, that no minute is made of it even in the log book; and but few men in war time can escape the above mode of punishment, particularly in those ships whose captains give that power to his inferior officers.

Gagging

This punishment is inflicted at the time of the offence being committed, which is generally for a seaman's daring to make a reply to his superior. The man is placed in a sitting position, with both his legs put in irons, and his hands secured behind him; his mouth is then forced open, and an iron bolt put across, well secured behind his head. A sentinel is placed over him with his drawn bayonet, and in this situation he remains, until the captain may think proper to release him, or until he is nearly exhausted.

To go through all the different modes of punishment resorted to in the British navy would be impossible, as almost every captain when appointed to a fresh ship, adopts new customs, with different ways to punish: and I have heard the captain say, when a man has been brought to the gangway to be flogged, and he has pleaded hard, by honestly stating that he did not know he was doing wrong, as it had been the customary order of the former captain: and what was the reply of this furious and unreasonable officer?

It was this—*"It was not my order, and I will flog every man of you, but I will break you in to my ways;"*—and he nearly kept his word, for within a short period of this time, upwards of three hundred men had been flogged or started, and this too whilst we were blockading an enemy's port. It is generally supposed that no man could be punished without having been guilty of some serious offence, but that is not always the case, for nineteen out of twenty men that are punished, suffer without being conscious that they have violated any law; and in many instances they are the most expert and able seamen: for instance—The fore, main and mizen-top-men are selected from the crew as the most sprightly and attentive to their duty; and yet those men are more frequently punished, and are always in dread when aloft lest they should be found fault with for not being quick enough, for punishment is sure to follow, and sure enough their conjectures are generally too true; for they are not only flogged, but their grog is stopped, or compelled to drink six or eight water grog for a certain length of time.

How many of those valuable seamen perished during the late war?

When aloft, and trembling from fear how many have actually fell from the yards and lost their lives, either on the decks or overboard; and how many hundreds have ran away, and by disguising themselves got over to America, leaving behind, perhaps, two or three years hard-earned pay and prize-money?

In this manner, together with those killed in battle, our ship was three times manned in a little less than seven years, for our complement of men was upwards of six hundred; and we had on our ship's books within that period twenty-one hundred; many of these men had purser's names—that is, fictitious ones, to avoid detection, in case they saw an opportunity to run away; and in most of those cases, their pay went to the droits of the Admiralty, as their relatives could not recover under a false name.

Observations on Impressment

This is a subject that has so often engaged the public attention, and is too grave a point, as a national question, for me to run a-board of; (and indeed it would be going beyond my original intentions) that I shall content myself with only relating some cases of impressment, to show the wanton extent to which it has by some commanders been carried; for the public being furnished with facts, will soon form an opinion, and should the legislature, in their wisdom, yield to the public appeal, this inhuman practice must soon give way to some more civilized system of manning the British navy, and stamp for it a name that will be imperishable.

The many cruel and heart-rending cases of impressment, which I have witnessed, both at sea and in harbour, are too many to stow away in this work, but I shall select two of a most wanton nature, which will show how that some men when vested with power can abuse it.

The first was, that whilst we lay at Flushing, in the year 1809. One day when the captain was on shore, the master hailed a transport, and not receiving a quick reply, he sent one of our boats alongside, manned and armed, to press the fellow he hailed, and who was not ready enough to answer.

When they had got on board, they found that the

crew had hid themselves in different parts of the ship on seeing a man-of-war's boat approach. The boat's crew were ordered to probe with their cutlasses in searching the ship, until they found him, and said they would take the whole crew unless he was forthcoming. Upon this they all made their appearance on deck, with the exception of this great offender. They each denied that they had answered the hail; but on search they found him who had.

They brought him on board, and he was compelled to serve for thirty-two shillings per month, whereas he was receiving five pounds ten shillings in the vessel he was pressed from. We had our full complement, and did not want a man; the reader, therefore, will pronounce what judgment he may think proper on such an outrageous act under the mask of authority.

The next that I shall relate is, that when we were convoying an East Indian fleet from England to the Tropic, one of them happening to have an excellent band on board, our captain took a fancy into his head that he would have some of them; so before he took leave of his convoy, he very kindly sent a lieutenant and boat's crew to press the two best musicians, which they did, and brought them on board, to increase our band, for the captain's amusement, and not to strengthen our force to engage an enemy.

It is not the purport of this work to propose plans for redress of grievances: I have pointed them out, and leave them to the wisdom of the superior powers to adopt the remedy. With the reader's leave, therefore, I will here drop anchor and come to.

End

Reviews

Morning Advertiser.

LONDON, WEDNESDAY, JANUARY 20, 1836. Price Sevenpence.

PROGRESS OF PUBLICATION.

Nautical Economy, or Forecastle Recollections of Events during the last War. By a SAILOR. W. Robinson, Staining-lane, Cheapside.

The principles of public liberty, diffused by the press, are now generally understood. We find persons of almost every grade in society ready and willing to assist in the overthrow of oppression, violence, and cruelty. The writer of this book, under a somewhat coarse name, seems to pursue a fair and praiseworthy object. He says in his preface:—"The order of the present day on land is Reform:—then why should the sea service retain its abuses?" The answer must be Reform by all means. The writer, in the hope of removing the disgust which the British seaman feels in the King's naval service, recommends reform, and gives a description (certainly not very new) of the shocking treatment to which men are obliged to submit in ships of war. The disgraceful system of discipline adopted by officers of cruel and despotic minds has produced an impression upon the seamen of England which can only be erased by legislative interference. Flogging and impressment degrade the national character, and the sooner the stigma is taken away the better.

A Committee of the House of Commons, composed of humane individuals (without one naval or military officer amongst its members), might prosecute inquiry into the present and past discipline of the navy, with a view of securing to the men fair and honourable treatment. Upon the Report of such a Committee much might be done to ameliorate the condition of seamen, upon whose courage and skill the country must rely in future wars. Under the present system of torture, and absolute slavery of the worst description, the men cannot respect their officers. They are goaded almost to madness, hatred, and mutiny. The author has served in the navy, and is therefore well acquainted with the proceedings on board a man-of-war. He does not propose a remedy for these grievances, but states facts. Every person who has been in the service must admit the correctness of many of the statements in this publication.

"Oh, protect the hardy tar,
Be mindful of his merit,
And when again you're plunged in war
He'll show his daring spirit."—— *Old Song.*

Naval & Military Gazette and Weekly Chronicle of the United Service
13 February 1836

Nautical Economy; or Forecastle Recollections of Events during the last War. By a Sailor politely called Jack Nasty Face. William Robinson.

The intention of the author is evidently to depreciate the Naval Service, to make the seamen discontented with their state, and to narrate incidents of no interest, solely for the purpose of introducing practices which have long been abolished afloat. We are only astonished that the writer could find a publisher. The book is undeserving of any notice. The "*Forecastle Recollections*" never could have been written by a thorough seaman; they carry with them every evidence as emanating from the mind of "a sea-lawyer," or "*Lord Mayor's man.*" "Jack Nasty Face" must, we opine, have hitherto filled the office of "*Jemmy Ducks,*" or a "*Jack in the Dust.*"

8.—THE EVENING NEWS, SATURDAY, APRIL 25 1936

Jack Nasty-Face Protests

LOWER-DECK DOCUMENT OF NELSON'S DAY

NEXT time I stand beside the Victory I shall scrap the sentiment and think instead of some of the bad things for which Nelson's flagship stood.

The other day there came into my hands a copy of a most remarkable piece of lower deck literature written exactly a hundred years ago in denunciation of the brutal autocracy of the Navy of Nelson's day. The quaintly worded title-page is worth reproducing in full:—

NAUTICAL ECONOMY
or
FORECASTLE RECOLLECTIONS
of
EVENTS DURING THE LAST WAR.
Dedicated
to the
BRAVE TARS OF OLD ENGLAND.
By A SAILOR,
POLITELY CALLED BY THE OFFICERS OF THE NAVY
JACK NASTY-FACE.

Be Ye Witness That I Lie Not.

Published By William Robinson,
9, Staining Lane, Wood Street,
Cheapside.
1836.

In his dedication "to my brother seamen and old shipmates," the author observes, "The order of the present day on land, it seems, is Reform: then why should the 'sea service' and its imperfections remain unattended to?"

A REFORM PIONEER

The identity of Jack Nasty-Face is presumably a mystery, but he was obviously a well-educated man for his time, who somehow strayed into the Navy and became one of the pioneers who brought about the betterment of conditions in the lower deck.

Describing his entrance into the Navy, he writes: "Whatever may be said about the boasted land of liberty, whenever a youth resorts to a receiving ship for shelter and hospitality he from that moment must take leave of liberty to speak or to act: he may think, but he must confine his thoughts to the hold of his mind."

The author entered the Navy on May 9, 1805. The recruits, after a medical examination, were battened down in the hold among the rats for the night. Thence they were transferred to another vessel at the Nore, where they were guarded by Marines with fixed bayonets in a hold which, in this case, was running not with rats, but with vermin. There they found articles of clothing, blankets, etc., were spirited away in an uncanny manner. Only later did they learn that members of the regular crew systematically robbed recruits by dropping lines fitted with fish-hooks into the abysmal gloom of the hold.

The ship's cook had the best job on the lower deck. He was often able to help himself to an extra allowance of rum, and as rum was used for the paying of debts, he was in clover. But a cook was subject to censure by his messmates if he served a bad meal, and justice was administered before a jury of cooks.

TYRANNY OF OFFICERS

Dealing with the tyranny of the officers, the author records: "We had a midshipman on board our ship of a wickedly mischievous disposition, whose delight it was to insult the feelings of the seamen and furnish pretexts to get them punished. This conduct made every man's life miserable that was under his orders. **He was a youth of not more than 12 or 13 years of age, but I have often seen him get on the carriage of a gun, call a man to him and kick him about the thighs, and with his fists would beat him about the head, and these, although prime seamen, dare not murmur."**

There follows a grim description at the delight of the crew when the boy officer was horribly killed by grapeshot in an engagement. "His death was hailed as a triumph over an enemy," we are told.

A vivid account is given of the author's nightmare journey from Gosport to London when returning on leave after the Battle of Trafalgar:—

"At Alton I was stopped by a party of soldiers, to whose inspection I had again to exhibit my ticket of leave; and then for 30 miles from the seaport was a poor seaman hunted by this detestable set, who are constantly watching, in the bye-lanes and fields, to intercept any seaman who may be coming that way. The inducement held out to these men-stealers is £5 for each seaman they may capture, and thus many a poor fellow is hunted by these bloodhounds. . . ."

IRON DISCIPLINE OF THE NAVY

Another example of the iron discipline of the Navy in Nelson's time is contained in the story of a sailor who asked leave to go ashore at Portsmouth, inventing the pretext that he wished to get married. The captain gave consent, but sent the luckless seaman ashore under escort of a sergeant and file of Marines to see that he did get married. The seaman resigned himself to having to ask every woman he met to marry him until he was accepted. It so happened that he was successful with the first woman he encountered. It is recorded that they were married at Kingston Church, and that the sailor left in his ship a few hours later without even knowing where his bride lived.

Descriptions of navel punishments make harrowing reading. At Spithead, in 1810, the author saw 200 lashes administered to each of four impressed seamen who had attempted to escape.

"The man is placed in a launch under the care of the master-at-arms and a doctor. There is a capstan bar rigged fore and aft, to which the poor fellow is lashed by his wrists, and for fear of hurting him—humane creatures!—there is a stocking put over each to prevent him from tearing the flesh off in his agonies." The ceremony of flogging through the Fleet is then described, the writer adding: "It often, nay, generally happens that Nature is unable to sustain it, and the poor fellow faints and sinks under it, although every kind method is made use of to enable him to bear it by pouring wine down his throat."

SAVAGE PUNISHMENT

"Starting," "gagging," and running the gauntlet are other savage punishments with which the author deals. The latter ordeal often meant that a man received as many as 600 lashes from yarn "nettles."

"Nineteen out of twenty men that are punished suffer without being conscious that they have violated any law, and in many instances they are most expert and able seamen," states the writer, who relates that in one short period while an enemy port was being blockaded upwards of 300 men were flogged or "started" on his ship alone.

Strangest of all to the eyes of 20th century "civilization," though, is an incidental passage in a description of the siege of Flushing, which refused to surrender. . . .

" . . . A second message was sent, requesting that the women and children might be sent away, as the intention was to bombard the town, and it was desirable that their lives should not be the sacrifice."—A.J.M.B.

Warrant Officers in Nelson's Day.

BLACKWATTLE

PRESS

To preview Blackwattle's documentary films
and podcast series
visit: www.blackwattlefilms.com.au

Printed in Great Britain
by Amazon

50099350R00076